PALETTE
mini
NUDE

First published and distributed by
viction:workshop ltd.

viction:ary™

viction:workshop ltd.
Unit C, 7/F, Seabright Plaza, 9-23 Shell Street,
North Point, Hong Kong SAR
Website: www.victionary.com
Email: we@victionary.com
🅕 @victionworkshop
🅞 @victionworkshop
Bē @victionary
🅟 @victionary

Edited and produced by viction:ary

Creative direction by Victor Cheung
Book design by viction:workshop ltd.
Typeset in NB International Pro from Neubau

ISBN 978-988-75665-1-9
Printed and bound in China

Michelangelo once said, "What spirit is so empty and blind, that it cannot recognise the fact that the foot is more noble than the shoe, and the skin more beautiful than the garment with which it is clothed?" Although nudity has been depicted throughout history across many fields such as the biomedical sciences, it remains restricted in most societies due to the social connotations and contexts in which it is open to misinterpretation. Yet, many artists have explored, celebrated, and featured it in their work, whether it be via painting, sculpture, or photography, as metaphors for complex contexts or simply to mirror life. This comes as no surprise, as nudity is part and parcel of the human experience that connects us all, regardless of age, gender, religion, or background.

With the progression of ideals, nudity may no longer be the big taboo it once was, but its depictions are still often treated with care and consideration. The nude palette has been an effective means in this regard, as its application connotes the diversities of humankind yet binds us together through a common and meaningful thread. Its range is at once subtle, revealing, and surprising due to its wide range of variations. As a testament to this, PANTONE's SkinTone colour guide is a compilation of 110 skin tones that was created by scientifically measuring them across a full spectrum of human skin types (PP. 154–159). It was specially formulated to be a physical representation of skin colours, in helping people like designers who often work with them in branding or graphics.

On that note, brands in the fashion, health, and beauty industries often use the nude palette to not only connect with their audiences on an intimate level by helping them relate with the brands' missions or stories better, but also to reflect the purity of the products through its soft and natural tones. STUDIO HOU's work for HINCE's 7th collection, featuring 'second skin foundations', demonstrates this (PP. 222–227), with its appealing choice of hues. Combined with a clever bottle design, which has a slightly slanted container shape and 'the most comfortable and appropriate angle' for using the pump, the distinctly modern and unique outcome makes a lasting impression. Similarly, Satomi Minoshima was inspired to translate the nuances around various skin colours by using bags as a metaphor through Skin Tote (PP. 160–177). According to Minoshima, 'our skin is essentially a container, and just like a bag, it contains the essence of who we are'. Along with her photography for the project, she sought to spread the aesthetic quality and diversity of skin colours through the stylish carriers. Count to Ten Studio's work on In One's Skin's range of nude watches also highlight the beauty of skin tones (PP. 136–141). Through the concept, product design, and packaging, the studio links diversity with the importance of social equality and harmony to foster co-existence in society.

In the modern art world, the possibilities of nude tones are truly endless. While many illustrators continue to draw naked figures in a variety of styles, there are those who also add a fun spin to the human face and form. Lundgren + Lindqvist's album cover design for Tentakel's 'TwoFace' features two drawings from artist EKTA (Daniel Götesson), juxtaposed to further demonstrate the duality suggested by the album's title (PP. 566–569). The back cover also apposes two typefaces to emphasise the idea, which are tied together by terracotta and beige shades that were derived from EKTA's original drawing papers.

In transcending boundaries creatively and in real life, the nude palette is a constant source of inspiration.

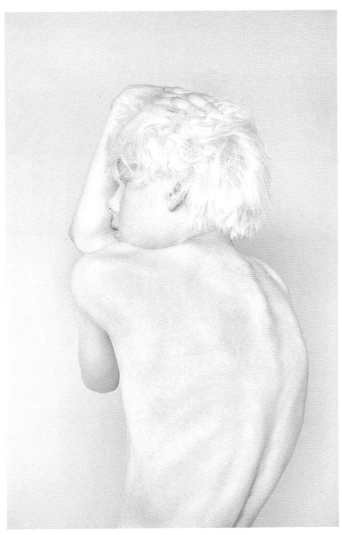

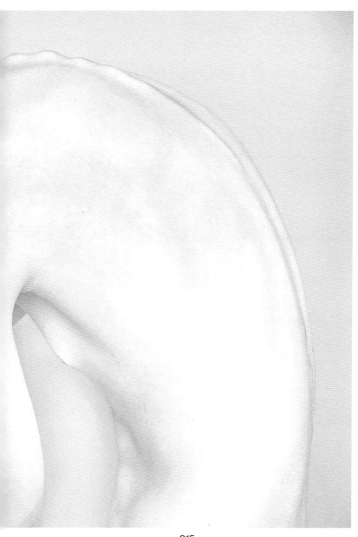

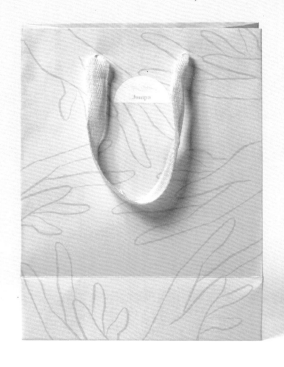

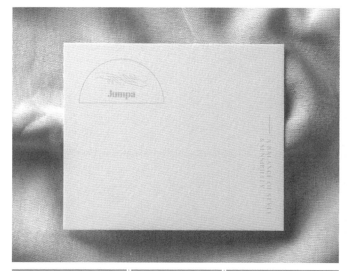

Coconut Milk
Lait de coco
950mL

Coconut Milk
Lait de coco
900mL

Paolo Massi	Founder
Telephone	+39 328 67 85 274
E-mail	paolo@okkaido.it
Website	okkaido.it

okkaido

okkaido

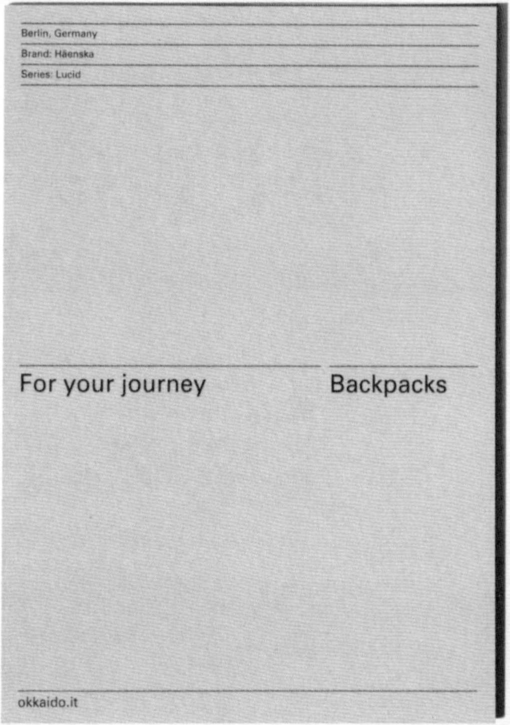

Berlin, Germany
Brand: Häenska
Series: Lucid

For your journey   Backpacks

THE
HANDSOME HAUS

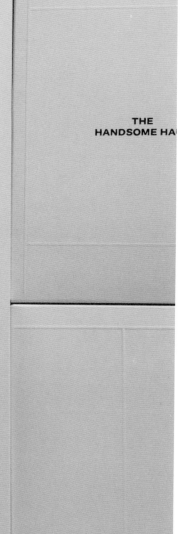

THE
HANDSOME HA

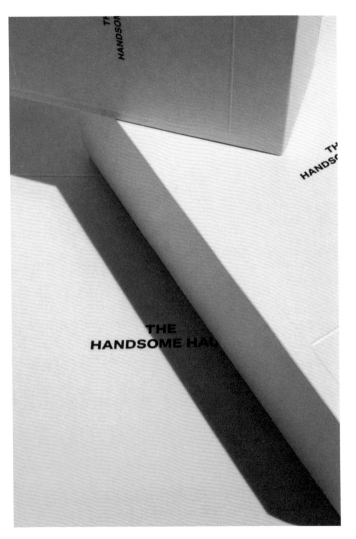

THE
HANDSOME HA

THE
HANDSOME HAUS

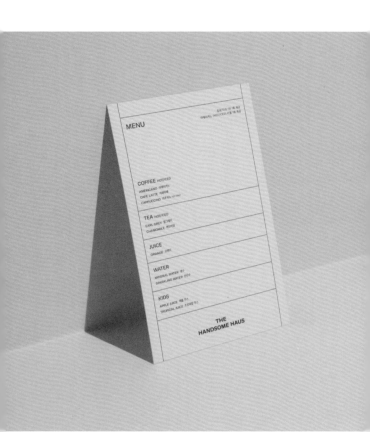

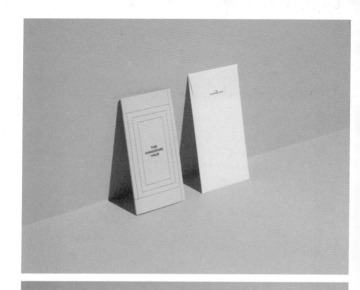

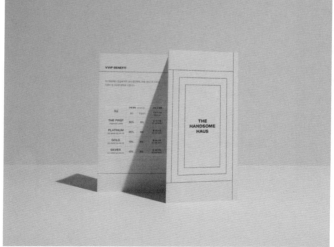

PRET**Z**IADA

stories

Our Number Six Reason for living in Sardinia is what I call Vanità Sarda, which loosely translates to Sardinian Vanity. What I mean by this is that Sardinians traditionally go the extra mile to create or to emanate beauty.

Nonna Annetta, Ivano's grandmother, had nine children. Her husband was a shepherd and would spend days out in the mountains with his herd of goats while she was solely responsible for the herd inside the house. She baked bread from scratch. She fed them food that she foraged for. She worked their clothes in the river that she walked to with ricotta urns which uphill on the top o was no running wa bathroom; there w She was a busy, man.

But every morni wake up, brush ou hair with care, bra ly and pin it into a Then she would c with a scarf so tha

ever see it and get on with her day's work.

Each woman in Sulcis had two hairstyles to choose from, *sa crocchia* and *is prettasa*. Below Tzia Beatrice graciously demonstrates how she styles her *is prettasa* every morning:

Vanità Sarda often has to do with personal aesthetics and is beautifully displayed in the regionally specific traditional dress. However it extends far beyond folklore. Sardinia has a generally rich tradition of decorating everything from bread to pocketknives. Living here, I try to find a daily reminder in the fact that no matter how tough life can be, it only takes a little dedication to find the beauty - the life-saving, superfluous beauty - in it all.

6 VANITY

Our Number Six Reason for living in Sardinia is what I call Vanità Sarda, which loosely translates to Sardinian Vanity. What I mean by this is that Sardinians traditionally go the extra mile to create or to emanate beauty.

Nonna Annetta, Ivano's grandmother, had nine children. Her husband was a shepherd and would spend days out in the mountains with his herd of goats while she was solely responsible for the herd inside the house. She baked bread from scratch. She fed them food that she foraged for. She worked their clothes in the river that she walked to with ricotta urns which uphill on the top o was no running wa bathroom; there w She was a busy, man.

But every morni wake up, brush ou hair with care, bra ly and pin it into a Then she would c with a scarf so tha

VANITY 7

ever see it and get on with her day's work.

Each woman in Sulcis had two hairstyles to choose from, *sa crocchia* and *is prettasa*. Below Tzia Beatrice graciously demonstrates how she styles her *is prettasa* every morning:

Vanità Sarda often has to do with personal aesthetics and is beautifully displayed in the regionally specific traditional dress. However it extends far beyond folklore. Sardinia has a generally rich tradition of decorating everything from bread to pocketknives. Living here, I try to find a daily reminder in the fact that no matter how tough life can be, it only takes a little dedication to find the beauty - the life-saving, superfluous beauty - in it all.

PRETTAXAS STORIES

Up until recently, each Sardinian bride brought with her into marriage a sort of dowry. In contrast to most of Europe, this dowry was considered property of the woman herself. With that right to own it, women came an equally important contribution of her own.

The dowry was expected to be prepared and created directly by her, and it was considered her contribution to the creation of her new home. Moreover, a direct expression of her skills and preparation. And, importantly, it was less of an offering to her future husband than proof of her obligation to help provide for her future family.

The difference, then, lay in that most of a woman's dowry was handmade by her for herself – not for her husband – and only what she wasn't able to make on her own (the ornately carved wooden chest to hold her linens, for example) would be bought as a gift for her from an artisan. This sort of self-sufficiency, the woman's provision of her own means to set up a new home, is at the heart of good Sardinian tradition. But she didn't carry a wide variety of attractive things and offering to decorate the impetuous of good Sardinian tradition.

The State Archives (of Cagliari & Sassari) contain detailed lists of marriageable dowries from Medieval times through the 1900's. And while there is no decorative vase ever listed in these archives, there was somewhere of a simple pitcher that would sit on the nightstand with drinking water inside. This pitcher was surely only one piece of a long list of ceramic pieces. Addition of pots, plates, and cups necessary to maintain one home.

Up until the 60's and 70's, every family had a collection of large ceramic urns with which they would gather the water from the town fountain or a nearby stream. But as plumbing slowly became more common in the cities and towns, they no longer served a practical purpose. Some potters could hold their techniques traditionally, while a handful of making their craftwork waste but, luckily, Sardinian crafts had a quick burst of recognition born in Italy in the early part of the 20th century. So, instead of creating an everyday urn, the "art" of creating them was transformed with an abundance of embellishments and decorations, as pictured here. The Nuptial Vase was transformed into the "art" of the landscape with abundance of embellishments.

The same abundance of embellishments, over-ornamented with an abundance of marble, ruffles and flourishes that grace the festival bread also grace the minutely embellished sweets which in turn graces the Nuptial Vase. It appears that the original pitcher given to new brides was much a simpler affair was embellished, over-ornamented, turned into a common gift for newly-wedded couples.

"Focused on organic beauty inspired by individual skin stories, Terrapi's nude, timeless colour palette strikes a balance between the feminine and the contemporary."

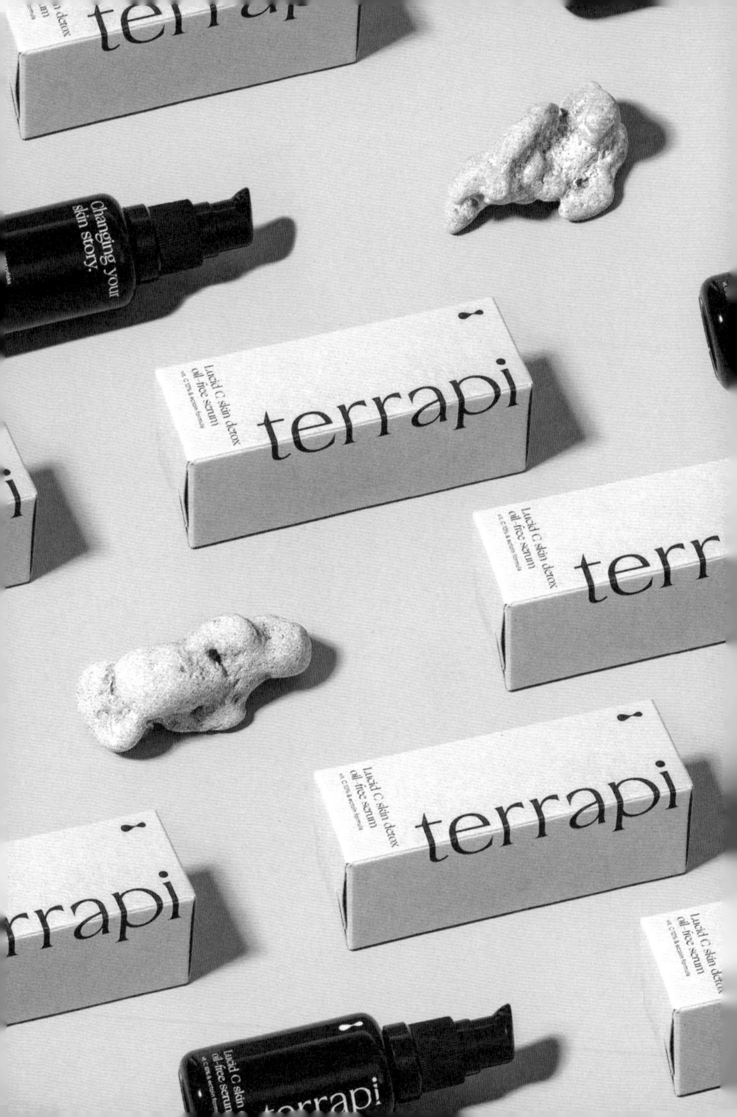
Changing your skin story.
terrapi
Lucid C skin detox
oil-free serum

terrapi

Lucid C skin detox
oil-free serum

vit. C 10% & ectoin formula

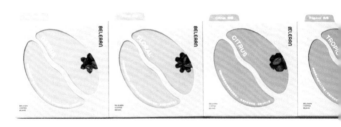

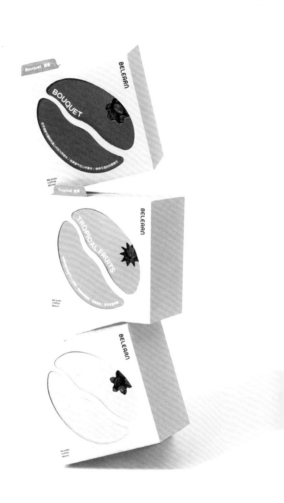

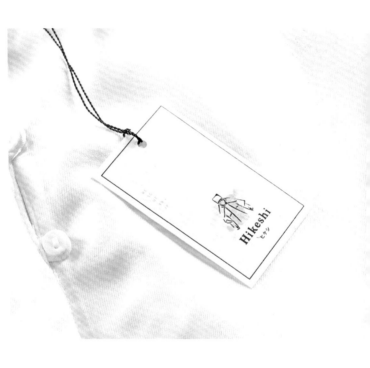

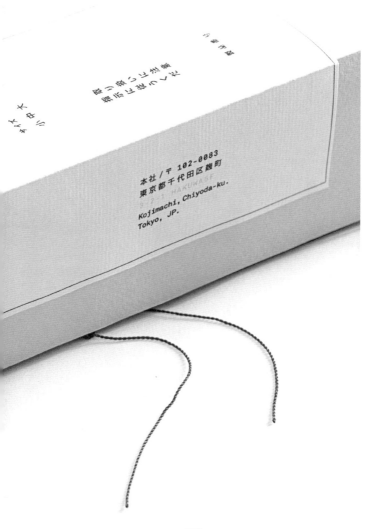

本社 / 〒 102-0083
東京都千代田区麹町
2-2-1 HAKUWA5F
Kojimachi, Chiyoda-ku.
Tokyo, JP.

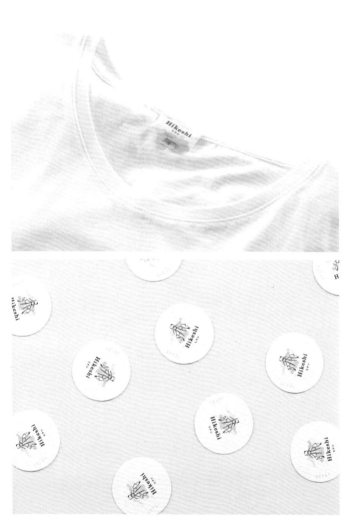

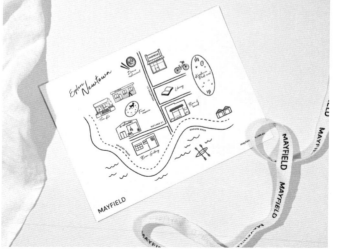

Artistic Director / Conductor
Chan Kah Mung

7

**Time is the Substance
I am Made of**
Huck Hodge
b.1977

for large mixed chorus and electronics
為大型混聲合唱團與電子音樂

All language is successive by nature
語言的本質是具有連貫性的

It is not effective for reasoning the eternal
是temporal

Time is the substance I am
時間是組成我的物質

MENY
MENOS E
IS

En la creació i balanceja d'un flasco, és important tenir en compte l'harmonia entre d'aquest, mitjançant un vidre, com a colorar els colors i la seva brillantor en relació amb la cara, els cabells i la tonalitat de la pell. L'equilibri entre l'ala i la essència, l'harmonia del conjunt, es un altre aspecte que reforça i elegància, igual que la remarca en la col·locació de la lligadura respecte a la tira pers ultil la de les espatlles.

Balanceja de consistència per la sofisticació i la simplicitat formal dels seus models. Els volums depurats, estilitzats, creats mitjançant formes molt simples, gairebé abstractes, es poden considerar escultures, que en alguns casos s'embelleixen gràcies a les característiques dels materials. Les lligadures completen la silueta de manera harmònica i, en molts casos, evitant els adorns, es remarca l'elegància de la simplicitat.

En la creació i contra la textura del seu conviccions s'en convida l'ús i la tonalitat de la s i y respecte al cre, al igual que a la línia de la col·locació.

Balanceja és format de pels i creant una mixta considerà esci a les característiques de manera considerà es remarca la s

ÉS MÉS
MÁS-LESS
ORE

es importante tener en
el conjunto y el rostro,
con la cara, en cabello
el aire y la corona, este
que refuerza la elegan-
del tocado respecto

posición y la simplicidad
epurados, estilizados,
abstractos, aspueden
se enfatizan gracias
ocasiones completan la
caso evitando adornos

When creating and choosing a hat, it is important to bear in mind
the harmony between the shape of the hat, the outfit and the face,
as well as its colours and sheen in relation to the face, hair and
complexion. The balance between the brim and the crown and
between them and the outfit is another aspect that heightens
elegance, as does symmetry in the position of the hat in relation
to the line of the eyes and of the shoulders.

Balenciaga is known for the sophistication and formal simplicity of his designs. The clean, stylised volumes created by means
of simple, almost abstract forms, can be considered sculptures.
In some cases emphasised thanks to the characteristics of the
materials. Headdresses complete the silhouette in a harmonious
manner and, in many cases, lack ornamentation, thereby enhanc-
ing the elegance of their simplicity.

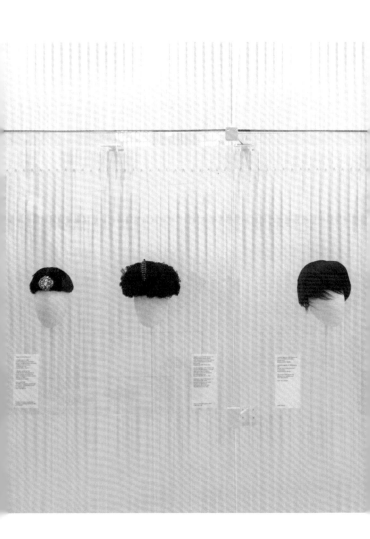

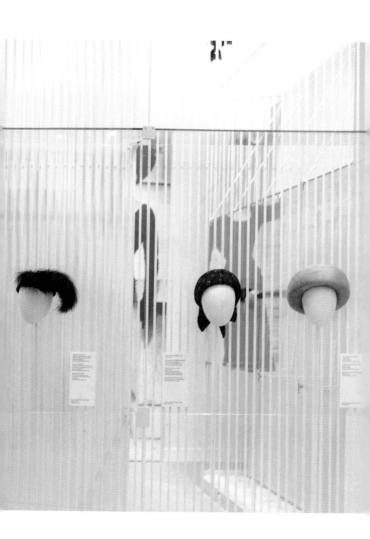

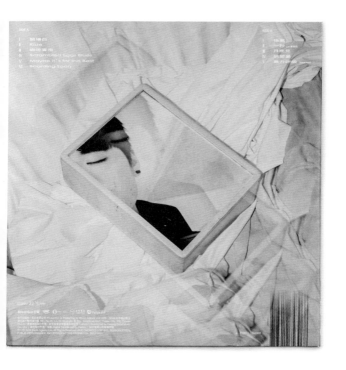

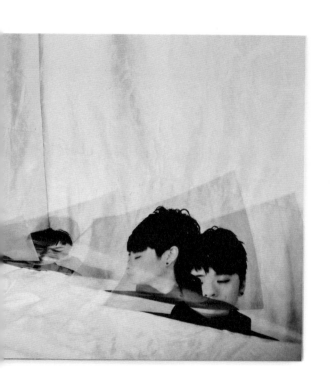

Scrambled Eggs
Scrambled Eggs
Blues

VII.

一秒 with 陳奕迅

IX. 青鳥飛魚

Smoke

X. 煙塵愛

Iris Palz-Konrad Mag.ª Dr.ⁱⁿ

Moserhofgasse 31
8010 Graz, Austria

+43 664 75 45 0111
therapie@palz-konrad.at
www.palz-konrad.at

ZU WISSEN, DASS
VERÄNDERUNG
MÖGLICH IST.
UND DER WUNSCH,
VERÄNDERUNGEN
VORZUNEHMEN.
DIES SIND
ZWEI GROSSE
ERSTE SCHRITTE

只要好好過日子

阿嚴 ——— 文．攝影

我們總習慣在失去後才去珍
惜眼前的這些，浪費許多時間摸
索追逐眼前的美味。

我們只是走在世間的那個，
不懂得享受了的樂趣
感受身一日的悲喜交好。

自己好了，
幸福，也不遠了。

"Through the symbolic use of colour and texture, the Melanie Auld packaging suite channels the fullness of life into physical form."

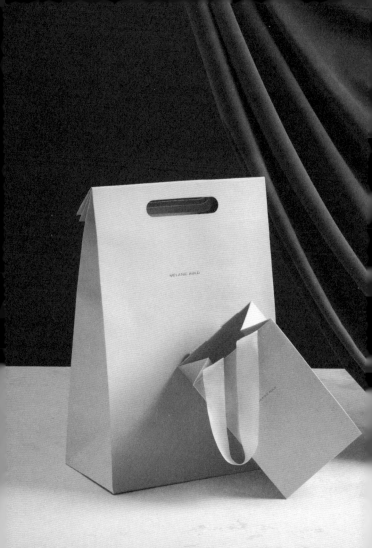

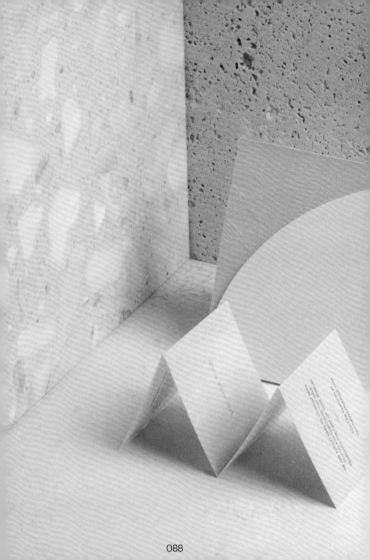

MELANIE AULD

MELANIEAULD.COM

LABECA

LONDON

Lara Ustumberk
+44 7770 69 89 29

LARA@LABECALONDON.COM
@LABECALONDON
LABECALONDON.COM

LABECA

LONDON

Bercis Gulec
+90 533 490 02 04

BERCIS@LABECALONDON.COM
@LABECALONDON
LABECALONDON.COM

LABECA

THE JOURNEY OF
COMFORTABLE & CHIC

THANK YOU FOR BEING PART
OF OUR JOURNEY AND FOR CHOOSING
LABECA FOR YOUR ADVENTURES.
YOUR TRUST MEANS THE WORLD TO US.
WE HOPE YOU LOVE AND ENJOY YOUR
CHIC AND COMFORTABLE PIECE
AS MUCH AS WE DO! DON'T FORGET TO
SHOW US HOW IT LOOKS AND
FOLLOW US TO KEEP IN TOUCH.

Lara & Bercis

@LABECALONDON
LABECALONDON.COM

LABECA

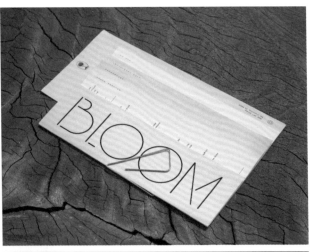

ABCDE
FGHIKLM
NOPQR
STUVW
XYZ

298 Alabama Street
San Francisco, CA 94110

GINGER
QUINOA
KOKOA
CACAO
CARROTS

298 Alabama Street
San Francisco, CA 94110

094

Giulietta Hextall
Ceramicist
+44 (0)7774 155 703
11 Crown Works, Temple St.
London, E2 6QQ
studio@giuliettahextall.com
www.giuliettahextall.com

Crown Works Pottery
Workshop and School

11 Crown Works, Temple St
London, E2 6QQ
info@crownworkspottery.com
www.crownworkspottery.com

Crown Works Pottery
Workshop and School

Giulietta Hextall
Ceramicist

Crown Works Pottery
Workshop and School

11 Crown Works, Temple St.
London, E2 6QQ
info@crownworkspottery.com
www.crownworkspottery.com

Giulietta Hextall
Ceramicist
+44 (0)7774 155 703
11 Crown Works, Temple St.
London, E2 6QQ
studio@giuliettahextall.com
www.giuliettahextall.com

11 Crown Works, Temple St.
London E2 6QQ
www.crownworkspottery.com

studio@giuliettahextall.com
www.giuliettahextall.com

Crown Works Pottery
Workshop and School

11 Crown Works, Temple St.
London, E2 6QQ
info@crownworkspottery.com
www.crownworkspottery.com

PINJA
FORSMAN

PINJA
FORSMAN

+358 40 821 4696
pinja@pinjaforsman.com
www.pinjaforsman.com

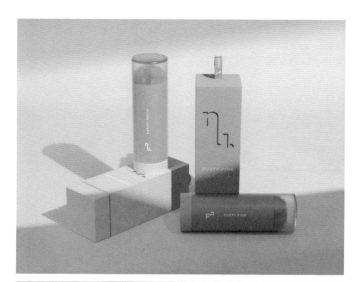

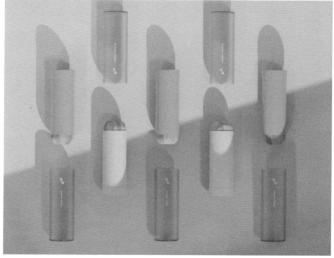

Hemos trabajado con la e...
tarea de dignificar la vida human...
a levantar un dique contra el oleaje...

Luis Barragán

P.6.

1.0

contacto@minna.com.mx
minna.com.mx

Av España 2019, Moderna
C.P. 44190 Guadalajara, Jal.
Mobiliario & interiorismo

MINNA
MOBILIARIO, LÁMPARAS E INTERIORES
ARTE VISUAL

MINNA 0001

Productos diseñados para motivar y generar emociones. Piezas creadas por manos mexicanas con materiales exclusivos de la más alta calidad.

1.0

MINNA

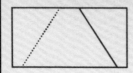

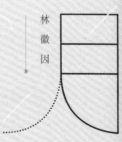

You are
the April of
this World

林徽因 著

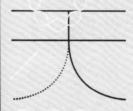

你间是的

人月天

四卷

文学

林徽因作品全集

The Complete Works
of Lin Huiyin

VOL. 1
Literature

Lin Huiyin

天津出版传媒集团
天津人民出版社

You are
the April of
this World

林徽因

著

建筑卷　四月天　人间的　你是

林徽因作品全集

The Complete Works
of Lin Huiyin

VOL. 2
Architecture

Lin Huiyin

天津出版传媒集团

天津人民出版社

你 是

林徽因作品全集

人 间 的

四 月 天

You are the April of this World

The Complete Works of Lin Huiyin

Lin Huiyin 林徽因

VOL. 1 文学卷　　VOL. 2 建筑卷

Literature　　　Architecture

天津出版传媒集团

天津人民出版社

你是人间的四月天

You are the April of this World

The Complete Works of Lin Huiyin

林徽因作品全集　林徽因

VOL. 1

VOL. 2

文学卷　Literature

建筑卷　Architecture

天津出版传媒集团

天津人民出版社

是

的

HAIR
SHAMPOO
(500ml) (GREEN LEAF)

7.KEY INGREDIENTS
SILK EXTRACT,

HOUTTUYNIA CORDATA
EXTRACT,

ACORUS CALAMUS
ROOT EXTRACT.

6.REPL...
PRODUCTS...
OILINESS...
REGULARL...
OUR LA...

4.PACKAGING
THE BOTTLE IS MADE
FROM ECO-FRIENDLY
PLASTIC, WHICH HAS
REDUCED THE USE OF
PLASTIC BY 30%.

LIFE GOES ON

HAND & BODY
LOTION
(500ml) (MOSS GARDEN)

8.HOW TO C...
APPLY TO SU...
AND MASSAG...
FULLY ABSOR...
THE DRY AN...

7.KEY INGREDIENTS
SILK EXTRACT,

MORINGA OLEIFERA
SEED EXTRACT,

HYDROLYZED
WHEAT PROTEIN,
SUNFLOWER
SEED OIL,
SHEA BUTTER.

4.PACKAGING
THE BOTTLE IS MADE
FROM ECO-FRIENDLY
PLASTIC, WHICH HAS
REDUCED THE USE OF
PLASTIC BY 30%.

LIFE GOES ON

CER

PLACE A D...
THE PRODU...
AND APPLY...
THE MOIST...
LENGTH AS...

LIFEGOeSON

LIFEGOeSON

TOOTHBRUSH
SET

3P   3 COLORS

TOOTHBRUSH
SET

3P   3 COLORS

1.YES TO.
RELIABLE QUALITY.
AN INTIMATE EXPERIENCE.
A CONSCIOUS PRACTICE.
AND NATURALLY DERIVED
INGREDIENTS.

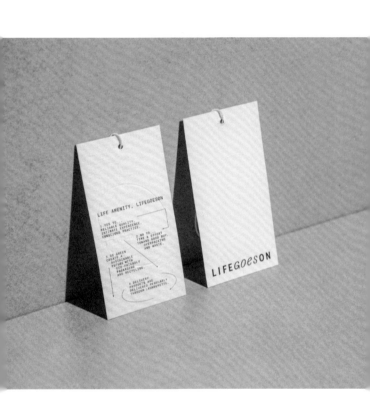

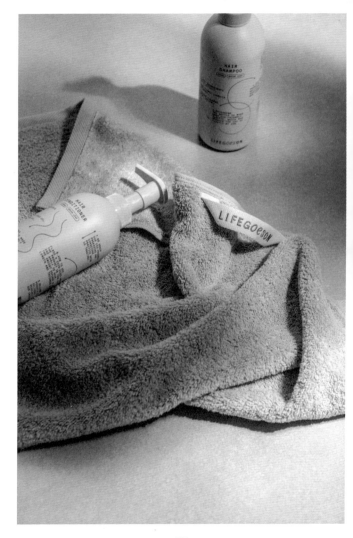

123

Annab

INTERIOR

Kerr

Annabel Kerr

INTERIOR DESIGN

IGN

INTERIOR DESIGN

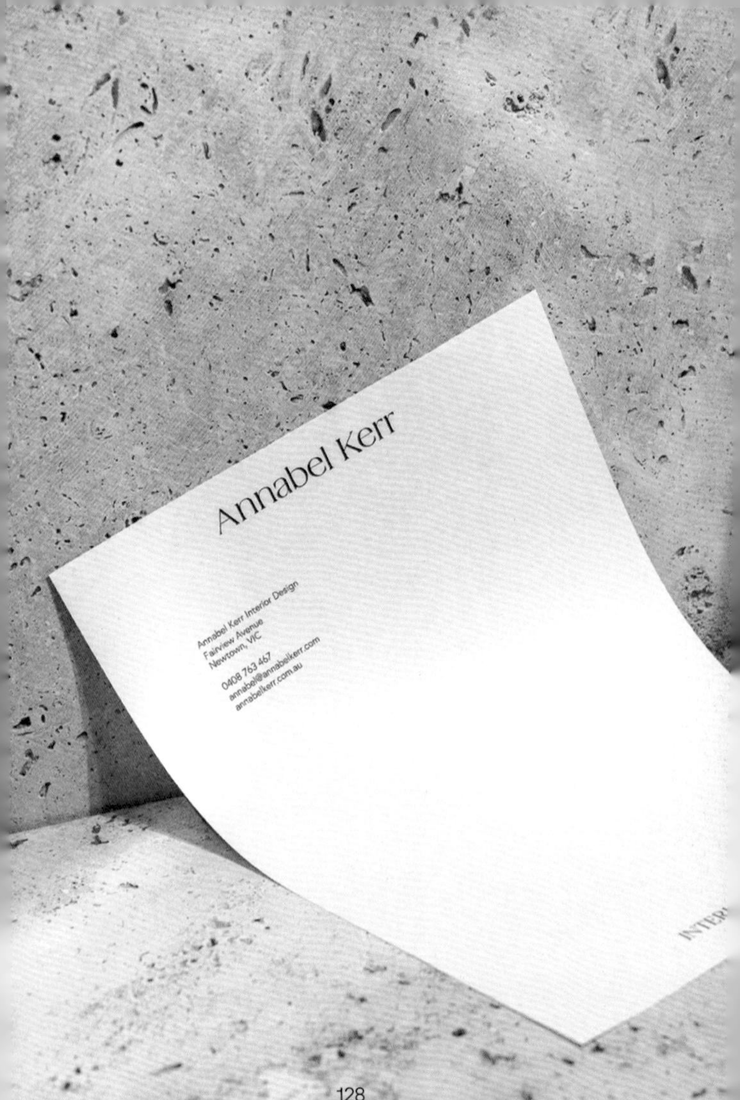

Annabel Kerr

Annabel Kerr Interior Design
Fairview Avenue
Newtown, VIC

0408 763 467
annabel@annabelkerr.com
annabelkerr.com.au

INTER

INTERIOR DESIGN

NYAMSUREN DASHZEVEG
Founder & Stylist

MOBILE +976 09561288
mail suree@thewayssheis.com
WEBSITE thewayssheis.com

Saving
THE WORLD
one booty at a time.

O·SIERY

137

DIFFERENT
COLOURS
SAME SPIRIT

 MORE®
HUGS
by Ken Lu

No4

Chernobyl area guidebook

№4 - the number of the exploded reactor
2020©

No4

Chernobyl

1986

4

20,000 mSv - death within hours of exposure

10,000 mSv - internal bleeding, death within 2 weeks of exposure

800-16,000 mSv - total radiation exposure of firemen and construction workers of Chernobyl

700 mSv - vomiting within hours of exposure

4 mSv - average yearly exposure level

0,1 mSv - chest X-ray

0,0001 mSv - eating a banana

a nuclear accident that occurred on Saturday 26 April 1986, at the No. 4 reactor in the Chernobyl Nuclear Power Plant, near the city of Pripyat in the north of the Ukrainian SSR.

Radiation level in Chernobyl area right after the explosion - 870 mSv/hour

Current average radiation level in Chernobyl area is 0.35 mSv/hour

* sievert (Sv) is a derived unit of measuring radiation dose

2020

Wildfire area - 470 km2

While the average radiation level remains normal, remnants of the exploded reactor under "the Arch" still expose thousands of mSvs. Currently it's impossible to utilize remnants of the reactor, however "the Arch" is able to prevent the leak of radioactive particles for the next 100 years until the tecnology is discovered.

Due to the years of desertion and recent wildfires, most of the buildings and tourist attractions are now in a poor condition. Most of them are not attended by guided tours anymore.

The Chernobyl zone is silently waiting for the new stage of its history.

In April 2020 Chernobyl zone faced series of wildfires. The fires were largely extinguished within two weeks, at least one suspect was arrested for alleged arson. The level of radiation remained normal, however the wildfires caused a major air pollution to the capital Kiev.

"Nude colours feel timeless, soothing and warm. It makes sense to think that it's in human nature to be attracted to this colour palette, as it's like a safe space."

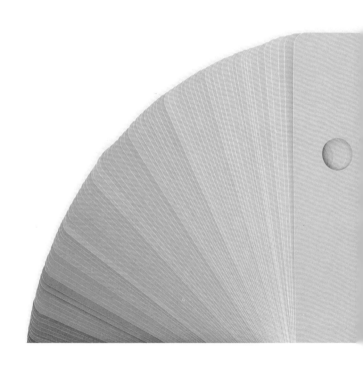

Index

To facilit
proces
PANTO
displ
in th
PA
th

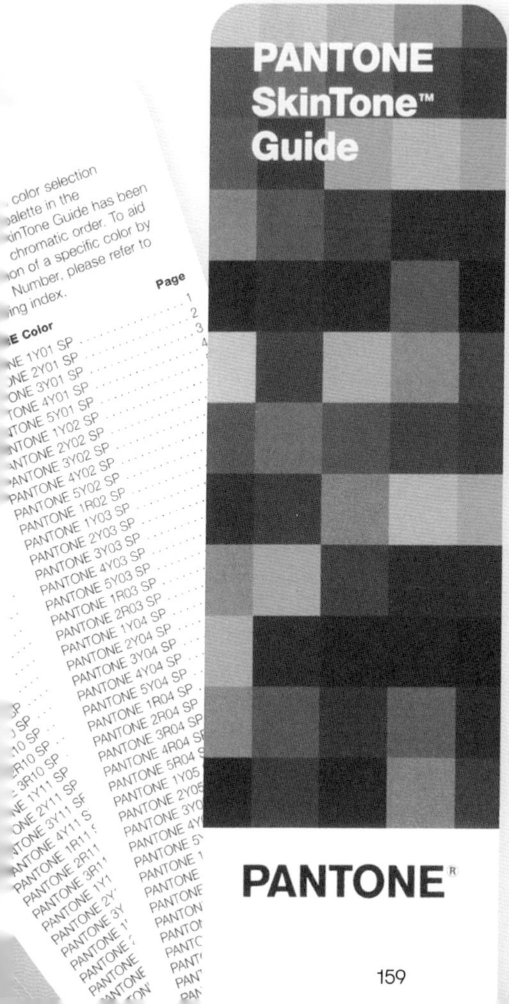

PANTONE
SkinTone™
Guide

PANTONE®

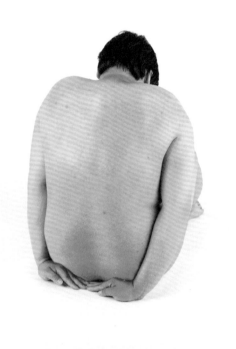

nude

organic underwear

Avinguda Diagonal, 320
Barcelona, Spain

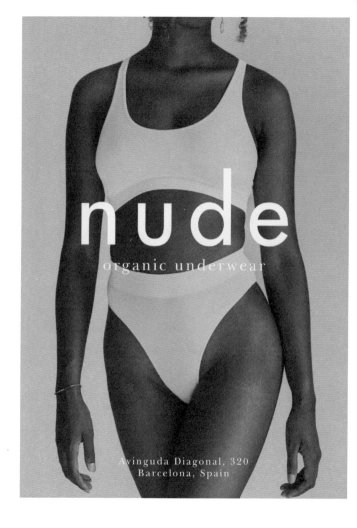

nude

organic underwear

Avinguda Diagonal, 320
Barcelona, Spain

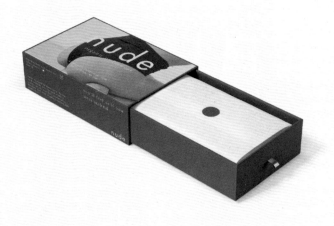

184

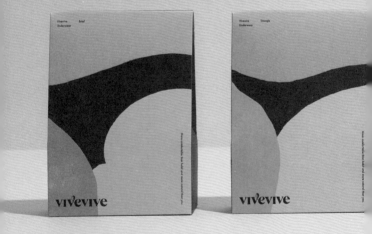

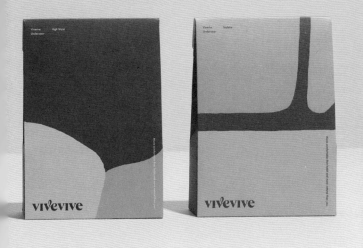

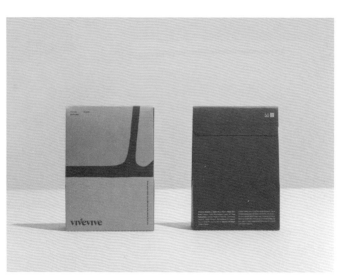

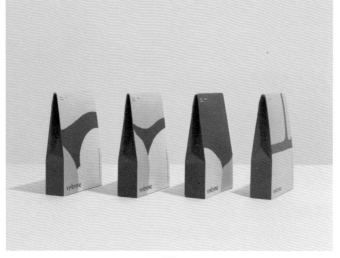

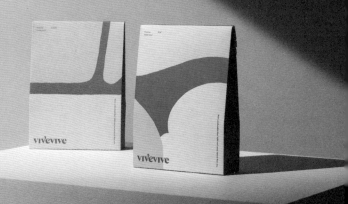

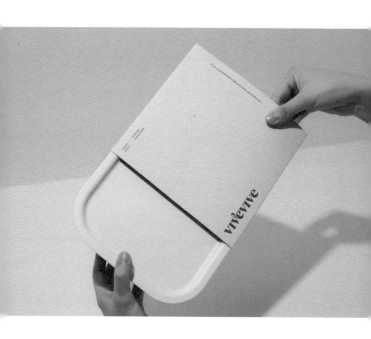

191

身体发肤
SHEN TI FA FU

身体髮膚

from _____

SHEN TI FA FU

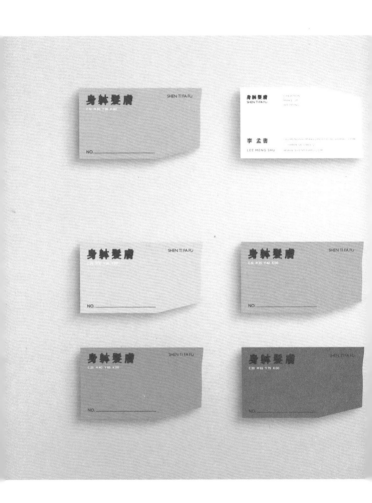

194

身体髮膚　　　　SHEN TI FA FU
C 22　M 37　Y 40　K 00

NO._____

身体髮膚　　　　SHEN TI FA FU
C 26　M 43　Y 52　K 00

NO._____

身体髮膚
C 50　M 67　Y 67　K 00

身体髮膚
C 57　M 77　Y 75　K 25

身躰髮膚　SHEN TI FA FU

NO.＿＿＿＿＿＿＿

SHEN TI
FA FU

NO.

Bring on

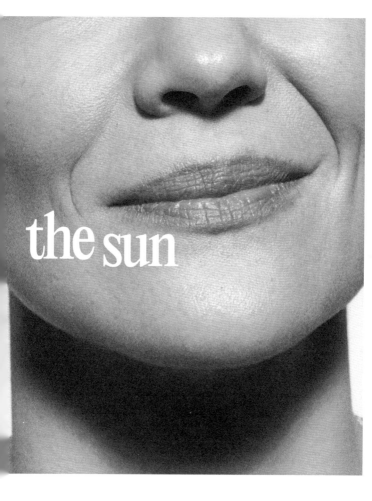

the sun

Bring on the sun

Bring on the sun

ace & tate

Our new sunglasses collection is out

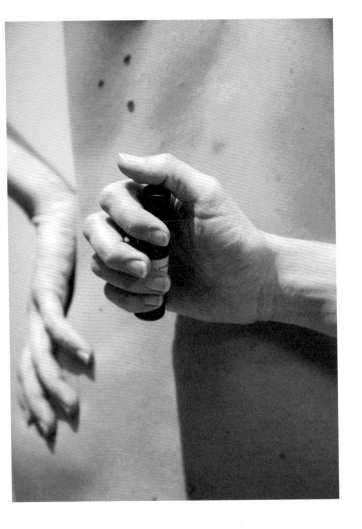

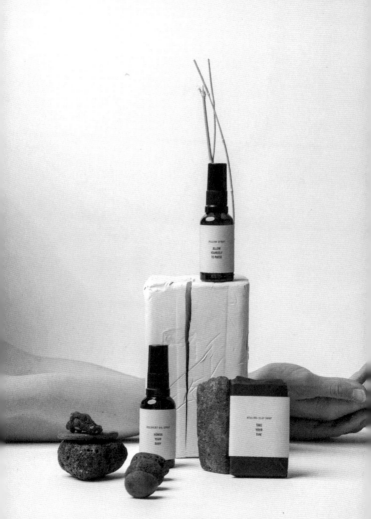

STRENGTH OIL ROLL ON

FOLLOW
YOUR
INTUITION

SOOTHING NIP&LIP BALM

PATIENCE IS KEY

SELF-CARE MESSAGE NO. P

HANG ON IN THERE

210

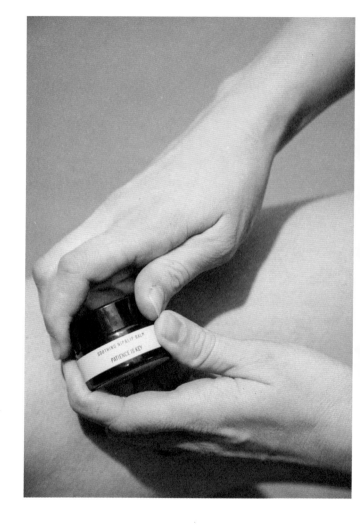

HEALING CLAY SOAP

TAKE
YOUR
TIME

STRENGTH OIL ROLL ON

FOLLOW
YOUR
INTUITION

213

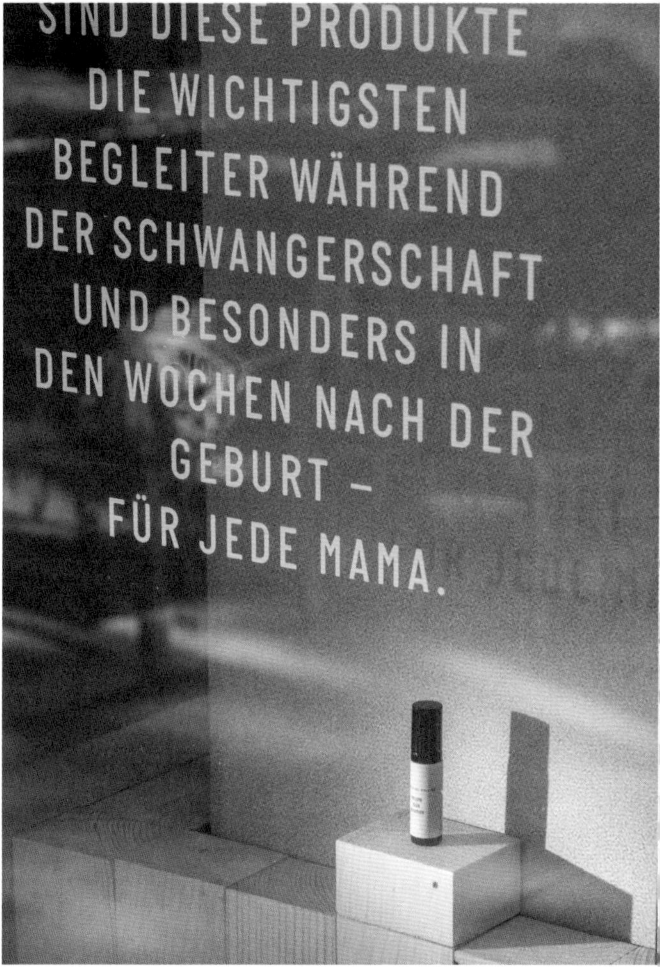

SIND DIESE PRODUKTE
DIE WICHTIGSTEN
BEGLEITER WÄHREND
DER SCHWANGERSCHAFT
UND BESONDERS IN
DEN WOCHEN NACH DER
GEBURT –
FÜR JEDE MAMA.

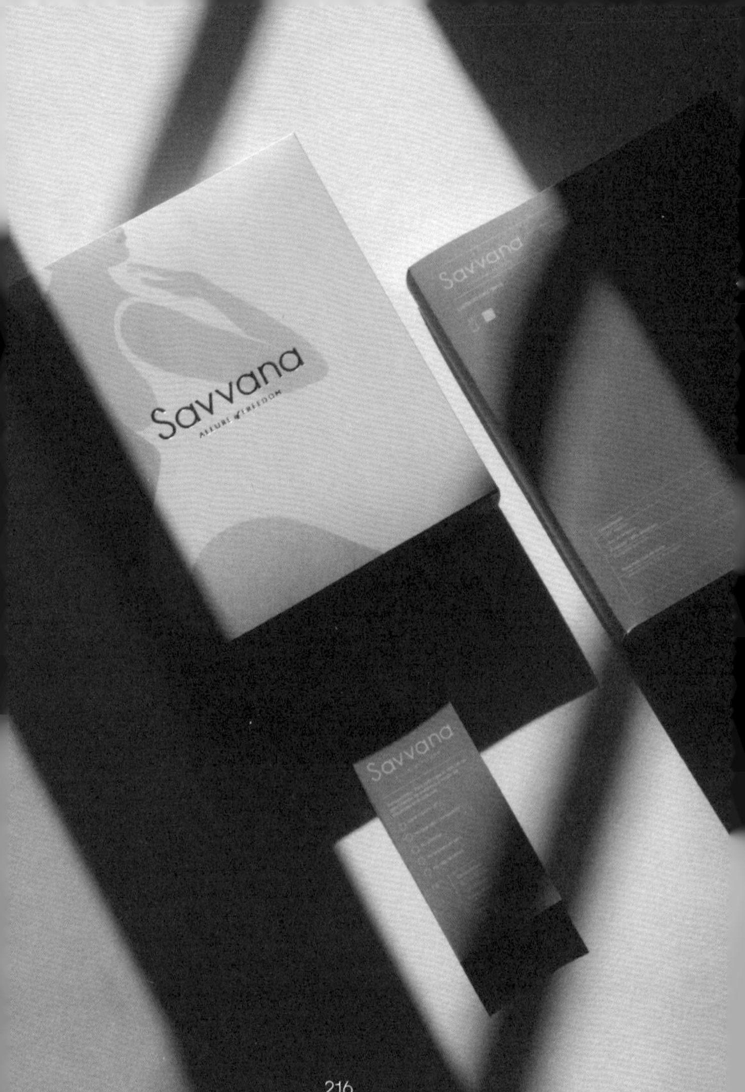
Savvana
Savvana
Savvana
Savvana

AUDREY VOLARIS
Founder
+33 (0)6 82 79 53 20
www.dirtyhandsstudio.co
contact@dirtyhandsstudio.co
DIRTY HANDS
CERAMIC STUDIO
Paris
@dirtyhandsstudio

"Nude colours were used because they are the most similar to our skin tones and familiar to us. Despite being a unique product, its colour palette is familiar and comforting."

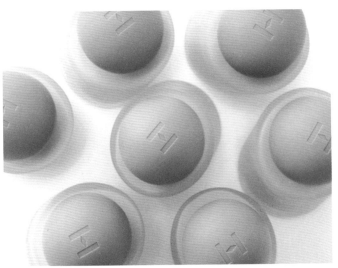

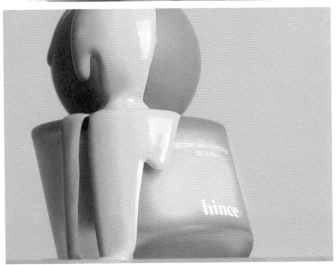

225

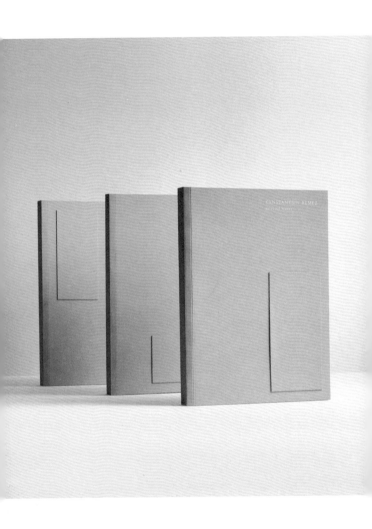

KANSTANTSIN REMEZ
selected works

231

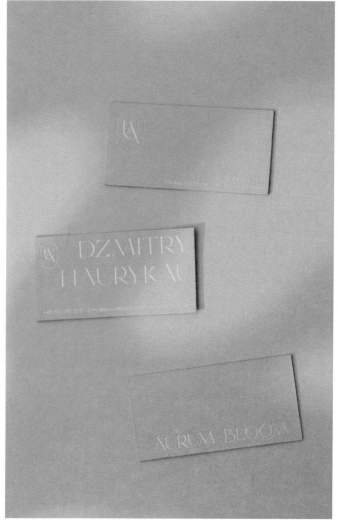

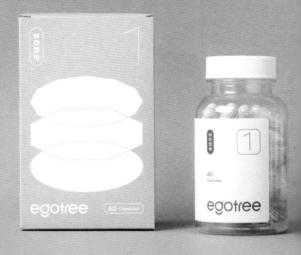

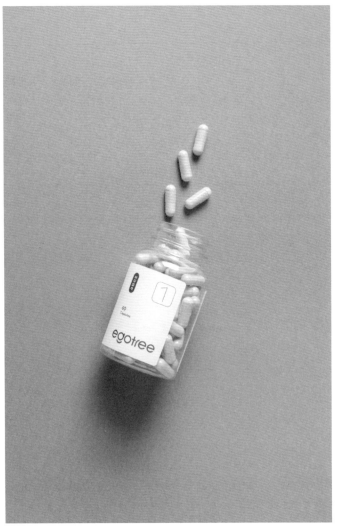

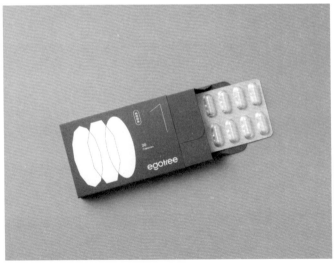

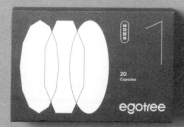

永
あ
ア
Ａ

游明朝体ファミリー
Yu Mincho Font Family
詳細へ→

製作文字的工作／文字を作る仕事　鳥海修

永あアＡ鳥海修

製作文字的工作／文字を作る仕事　鳥海修

Sanseido 27

解説

理想の文字とは何か？　永
フォント制作会社「字游工房

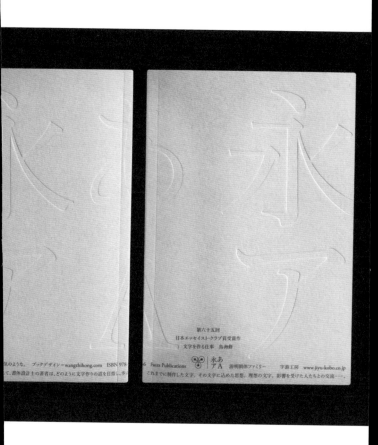

第六十五回
日本エッセイスト・クラブ賞受賞作
文字を作る仕事　鳥海修

これまでに制作した文字。その文字に込めた思想。理想の文字。影響を受けた人たちとの交流……。

気のような。　ブックデザイン＝wangzhihong.com　ISBN 978

て、書体設計士の著者は、どのように文字作りの道を目指し、歩

6　Faces Publications　　永あ／ア A　游明朝体ファミリー　　字游工房　www.jiyu-kobo.co.jp

OROTON

OROTON.COM

ORC

TON

261

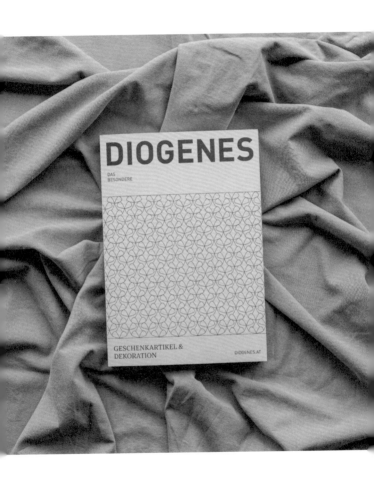

DIOGENES

DAS
BESONDERE

GESCHENKARTIKEL &
DEKORATION

DIOGENES.AT

FRISEURSALON
CHRISTINA PETER

MÜHLSTR. 22/1
88348 BAD SAULGAU
07581 / 534 5505

WWW.CHRISTINA-PETER.DE

CHRISTINA PETER
FRISEURSALON

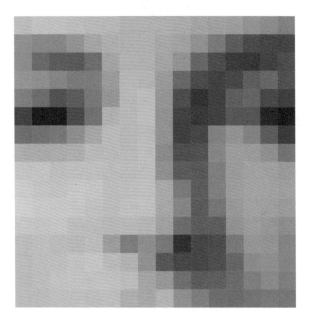

éssers.

10 de desembre
Commemoració de la Declaració
Universal dels Drets Humans
València, ciutat igual, ciutat justa

 AJUNTAMENT
DE VALÈNCIA

éssers.

10 de desembre
Commemoració de la Declaració
Universal dels Drets Humans

València, ciutat igual, ciutat justa

 AJUNTAMENT
DE VALÈNCIA

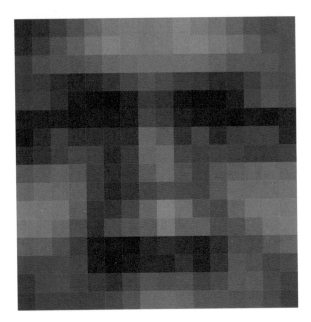

éssers.

10 de desembre
Commemoració de la Declaració
Universal dels Drets Humans

València, ciutat igual, ciutat justa

 AJUNTAMENT
DE VALÈNCIA

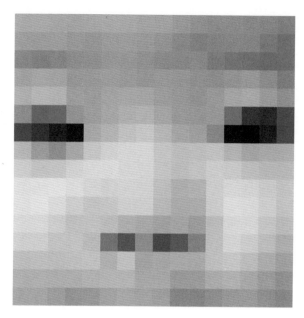

éssers.

10 de desembre
Commemoració de la Declaració
Universal dels Drets Humans

València, ciutat igual, ciutat justa

AJUNTAMENT
DE VALÈNCIA

éssers.

10 de desembre
Commemoració de la Declaració
Universal dels Drets Humans

València, ciutat igual, ciutat justa

 AJUNTAMENT
DE VALÈNCIA

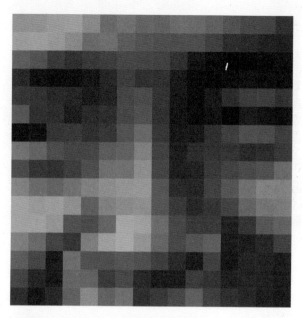

éssers.

10 de desembre
Commemoració de la Declaració
Universal dels Drets Humans

València, ciutat igual, ciutat justa

 AJUNTAMENT
DE VALÈNCIA

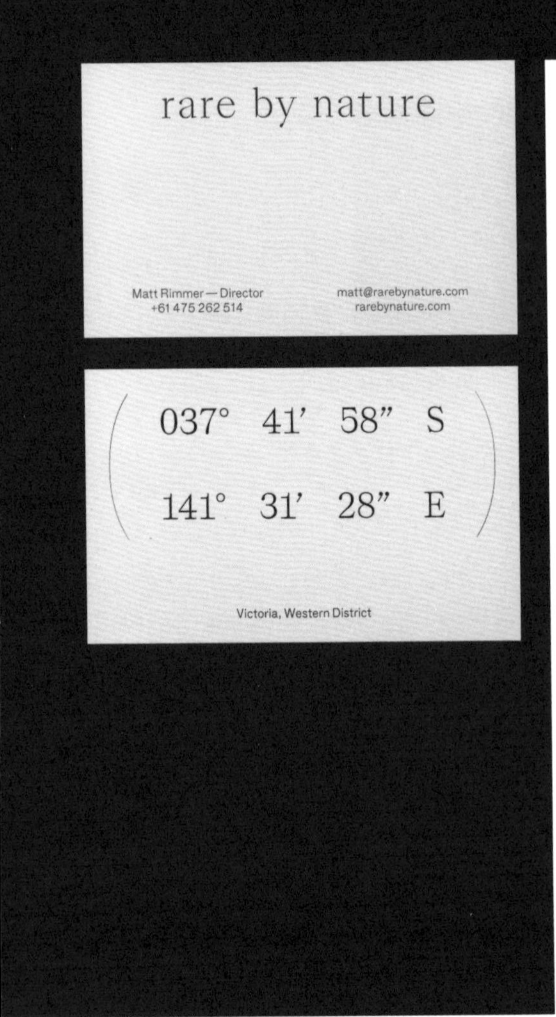

rare by nature

Matt Rimmer — Director
+61 475 262 514

matt@rarebynature.com
rarebynature.com

$$(\quad 037° \quad 41' \quad 58" \quad S$$

$$141° \quad 31' \quad 28" \quad E \quad)$$

Victoria, Western District

SINGLE ORIGIN: / ac
beauty staple. ② Tak
against oxidative stres

Grown within a single geographic origin. ① Placenta extracts have long been a traditional upplementally, animal placentas may help to reduce UV aging effects. ③ May also protect

rare by nature

rare by nature

Australian Sheep Placenta.
100% Western Victoria Merino

SINGLE ORIGIN: / adj / Grown within a single geographic
origin. ① Placenta extracts have long been a staple
beauty staple. ② Taken supplementally, animal placenta
may help to reduce UV aging effects. ③ May also protect
against oxidative stress.

LARS WALLIN   AVKLÄDD

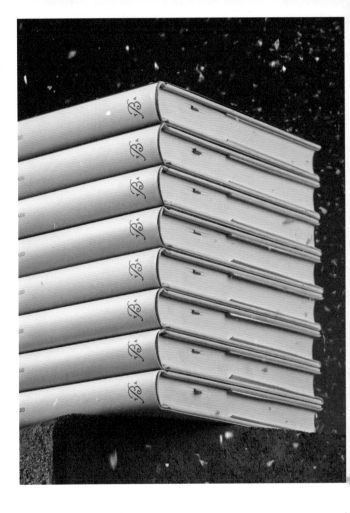

283

No.171

No.172

No.173

No.174

No.172
Make
Me
Bio.
Formuła dla sprężystości
każdego rodzaju cery
No.173
No.172
Olej z pestek moreli
Olej z pestek malin
Masło shea
Olejek arganowy
No.171

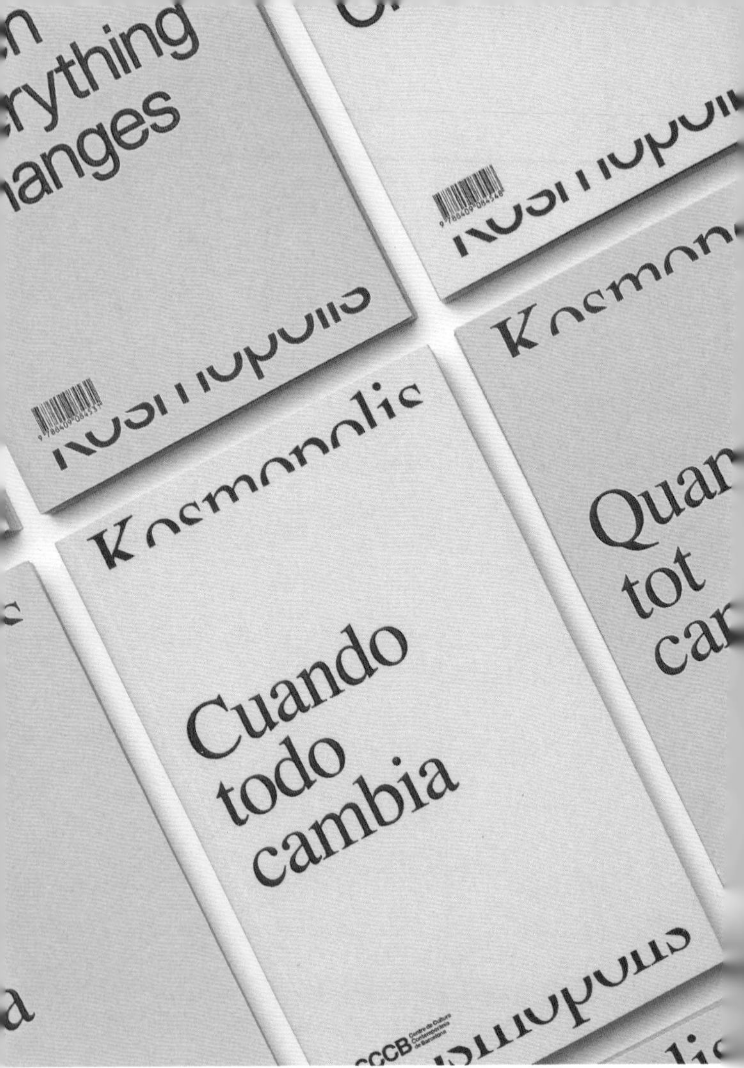
Cuando
todo
cambia

When
Everything
Changes

Kosmopolis

CCB Centre de Cultura
Contemporània
de Barcelona

Quan
tot

Kosmopolis

Quan
tot
canvia

Quan tot canvia | When Everything Changes

CCCB Centre de Cultura
Contemporània
de Barcelona

Cuando
todo
cambia

Cuando todo cambia |

CCCB Centre de Cultura
Contemporània
de Barcelona

05

The Family Is Dead,
Long Live the Family
Conversation between Orna Donath,
Maria Llopis and Brigitte Vasallo,
moderated by Bel Olid

CONCLUSIÓ
CONVERTIR LES DADES EN UN SERVEI PÚBLIC

No hauríem d'obligar les empreses de l'interneteo digital a compartir dades esenciales pels seus algoritmos, per tal de convertir-lo en un servei públic, per garantir-ne l'accés? Si les dades agregades són de domini públic, per evitar un poder arbitrari o uns poders dominants, ja sigui públic de les dades equilibrats als monopolis sorgintesse...

Plantejar un debat sobre aquest tema no val dir que tota societat digital. Com li n'espantosa conversa de les digital, aparto però encall: per un debat públic sobre l'impacte de la intel·ligència artificial i el dir que tots temensticia, el valor els beneficis que es deriven d'a societat tan sols sigui a càrrec del debat per reflexionar sobre el bé que estem creant en millor que es pot en present.

No hauríe d'obligar que ens trobem en la primera fase de debat del futur model de societat digital. Què fem i com les tasa es agru primera fase de debat és de la societat digital total ens implesca construïr en el futur...

114

09

Werner
Herzog/
Paul
Holden-
gräber

"There is a sense of refinement, calmness, and luxury in natural colours that draws each one of us in, one way or another."

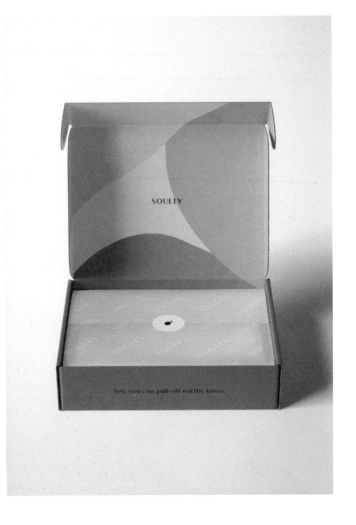

303

313

320

objects
essential living

Poetic objects
for essential living

forsstudio.com

forsstudio.com

Poetic objects
for essential living

2 LARGE CUPS

☐ WHITE | FLCU-W-2   ☐ ROSE | FLCU-R-2
| FLCU-G-2

forsstudio.com

forsstudio.com

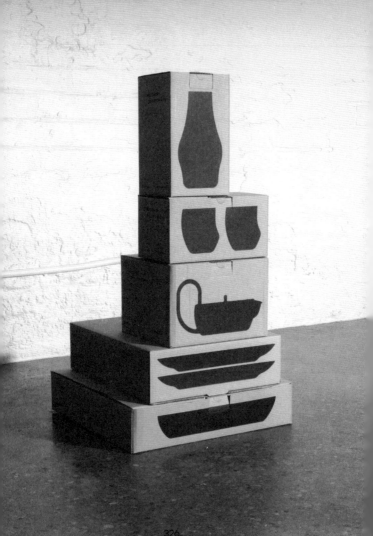

poetic objects
for *essential living*

førs

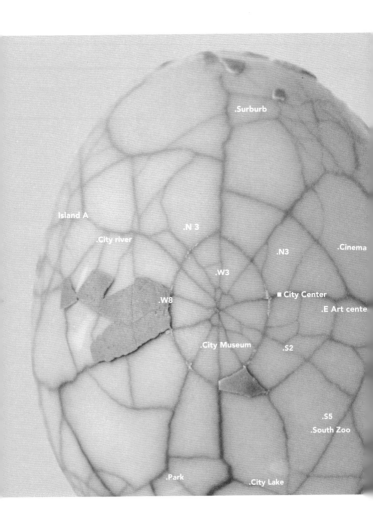

.Surburb

Island A

.City river

.N 3

.N3

.Cinema

.W3

.W8

■ City Center

.E Art cente

.City Museum

.S2

.S5

.South Zoo

.Park

.City Lake

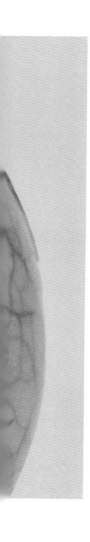

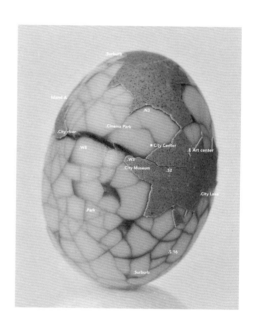

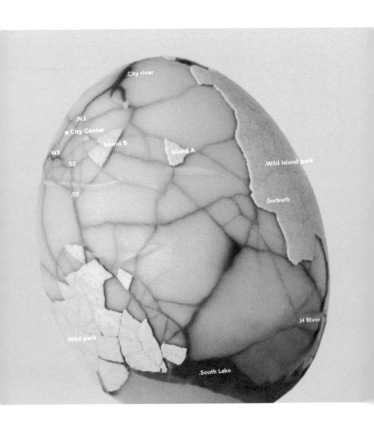

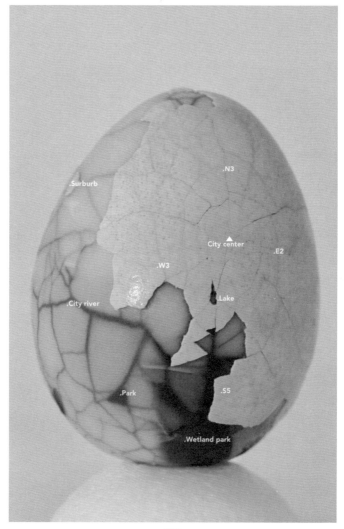

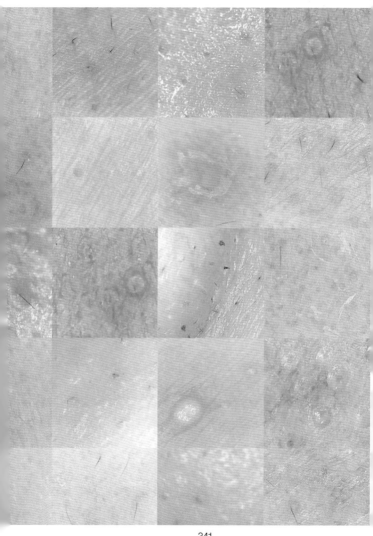

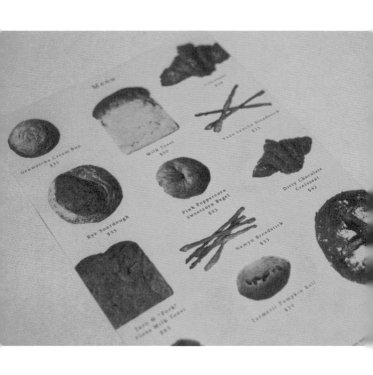

Menu

Genmaicha Cream Bun
$35

Milk Toast
$50

Yuzu Shichu Breadstick
$35

Dirty Chocolate
Croissant
$42

Rye Sourdough
$55

Pink Peppercorn
Sweetcorn Bagel
$35

Namyu Breadstick
$35

Taro & "Pork"
Floss Milk Toast
$45

Turmeric Pumpkin Roll
$30

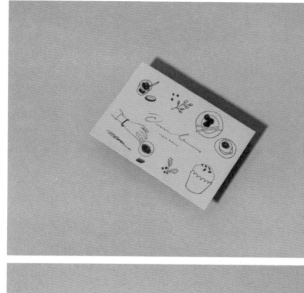

sow to seed

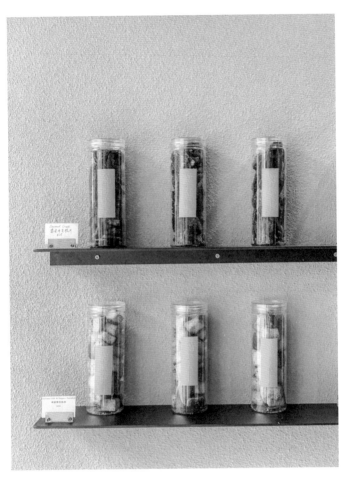

vegan bakery

Pitta² volumising
conditioner by

CHĀMPO

formulated for fine
or thinning hair that
yearns for fullness
and body.

250ml/9.2 fl.oz.℮

Pitta volumising
shampoo by

CHĀMPO

formulated for fine
thinning hair that
ns for fullness
dy.

2 fl.oz. ℮

Vata, Pitta and Kapha are
doshas. Much like star signs,
they are expressions of you
and your hair, helping to
identify its character traits
so you can tailor haircare
to your needs.
Discover your hair

champoh

Pittal volumising
shampoo by

CHĀMPO

formulated for fine
or thinning hair that
yearns for fullness
and body.

260ml/9.2 fl.oz. ℮

Vata¹ hydrating
shampoo by

CHAMPO

formulated for dry,
difficult or damaged
hair that longs for
moisture.

260ml/9.2 fl.oz. ℮

"The nude colour palette was inspired by the natural tones of the pottery clays. The two nude colours can both contrast and complement each other at the same time."

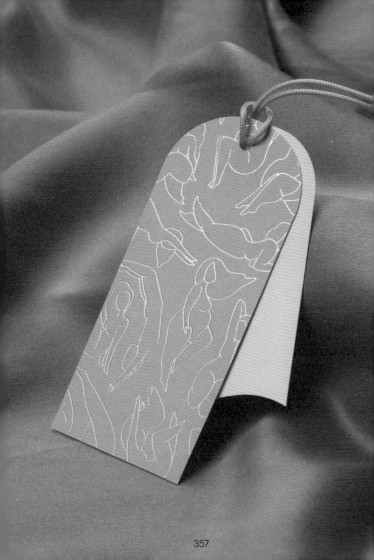

WOMEN IN MIND

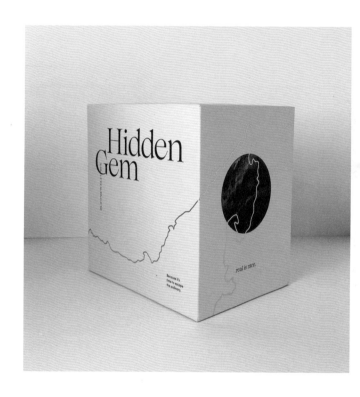

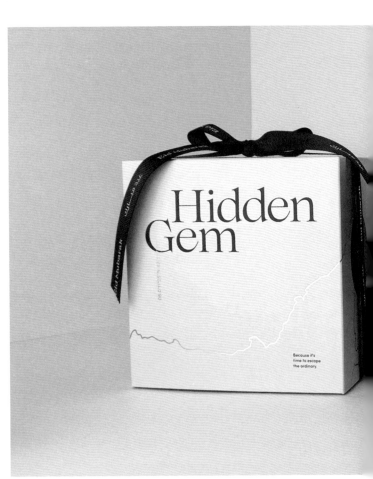

We usually say it's handcrafted, but
actually it comes from the heart

Valérie Coffe

Esthétique,
Visage et Corps.

¹ Traitement Professionnel Soluble, sans Perçage, 100% Vegan et sans Produits Nocifs. Les ongles sont protégés et regénérés.

Ongles Bio-Sculpture¹

Pose VSP* : Main ou Pieds (soin inclus) – 1H	35€
Forfait VSP* : Mains et Pieds (soin inclus) – 2H	60€
Pose gel : Main ou Pieds (soin inclus) –1H30min	40€
Pose gel avec extensions – 2H	60€
Dépose seul VSP* ou gel– 30min	15€
Pose vernis classique	15€

Maquillage

Jour naturel ou Soir sophistiqué	25-35€
Mariée (essai inclus)	60€
Cours d'auto-maquillage	60€
Pose faux cils	15€
Extension de cils (cils à cils– 1H45min	80€
Extension volume (2D à 8D) –2H	120-140€
Réhaussils (teinture et recourbement)	35€
Structure du sourcil	25€

Épilation

Sourcils/Lèvres	9€
Aisselles/Maillot (simple)	12€
Maillot Semi-Intégral/Intégral	18-25€
Demi-Jambes/Bras/Cuisses	15€
¾ Jambes	20€
Jambes (complètes)	24€

*VSP : Vernis semi-permanent

Soin, (Produits BIO)
Visage et Corps.

Soin Visage

Soin visage (nettoyant de peau classique) – 1H	40€
Soin visage anti-âge –1H30min	55€

Soin Corps

Gommage corps –30min	35€
Gommage : Corps et Enveloppement (peau de soie) –1H	50€
Gommage : Mains ou Pieds – 20min	15€
Massage relaxant (californien ou pierres chaudes) –1H	60€
Massage : Dos ou Jambes lourdes –20min	25€

Événementiel, Atelier.
(Chez moi ou chez vous)

Anniversaire & Enterrement de Vie de Jeune Fille
Atelier maquillage & soins corporels : conseils, cours d'auto-maquillage, massages etc...
Personnalisation de la prestation « Devis sur demande

Coaching en image
Conseil maquillage, coiffure & look selon la morphologie et personnalité de chacun.
Personnalisation de la prestation « Devis sur demande

Prestation "Ongles Bio-Sculpture" en supplément avec...

Graphique : 3136G
3684 av. du Champs-de-Foire.

Tél. : +31 (0)1 21 14 34 53
Mail : valerie.coffe@gmail.com

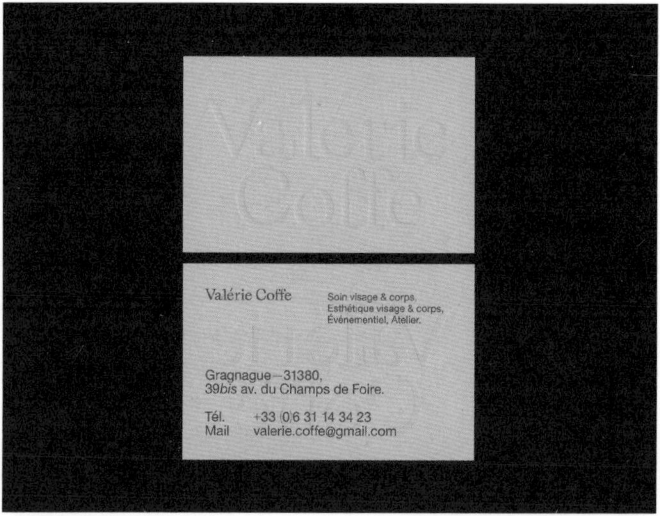

Valérie Coffe

Soin visage & corps.
Esthétique visage & corps,
Événementiel, Atelier.

Gragnague—31380,
39*bis* av. du Champs de Foire.

Tél.   +33 |0|6 31 14 34 23
Mail   valerie.coffe@gmail.com

Valérie Coffe

Soin visage & corps.
Esthétique visage & corps,
Événementiel, Atelier.

Gragnague—31380,
39bis av. du Champs de Foire.

Tél.   +33 |0|6 31 14 34 23
Mail   valerie.coffe@gmail.com

371

Johanna Juhlin — Senior Associate + Advokat
(Office) 0046 107 223 633
(Direct) 0046 703 882 458
(Email) johanna.juhlin@morrislaw.se

Advokatfirman Morris AB
Göteborg: Vallgatan 30, 411 16 Göteborg, Sweden
Stockholm: Hamngatan 13, 111 47 Stockholm, Sweden
✉ ⟶ Box 3442, 103 69 Stockholm, Sweden

MORRISLAW.SE

Linda Dahlström — Senior Associate + Advokat
(Office) 0046 107 223 614
(Direct) 0046 738 264 772
(Email) linda.dahlstrom@morrislaw.se

Advokatfirman Morris AB
Göteborg: Vallgatan 30, 411 16 Göteborg, Sweden
Stockholm: Hamngatan 13, 111 47 Stockholm, Sweden
✉ ⟶ Box 3442, 103 69 Stockholm, Sweden

MORRISLAW.SE

Martin Taranger — CEO
(Office) 0046 107 223 62
(Direct) 0046 707 821 28
(Email) martin.taranger@
Advokatfirman Morris AB
Göteborg: Vallgatan 30,
Stockholm: Hamngatan
✉ ⟶ Box 3442, 10

MORRISLAW.SE

Nils Olofsson — Senior Associate + Advokat
(Office) 0046 107 223 622
(Direct) 0046 707 104 220
(Email) nils.olofsson@morrislaw.se

Advokatfirman Morris AB
Göteborg: Vallgatan 30, 411 16 Göteborg, Sweden
Stockholm: Hamngatan 13, 111 47 Stockholm, Sweden
✉ ⟶ Box 3442, 103 69 Stockholm, Sweden

MORRISLAW.SE

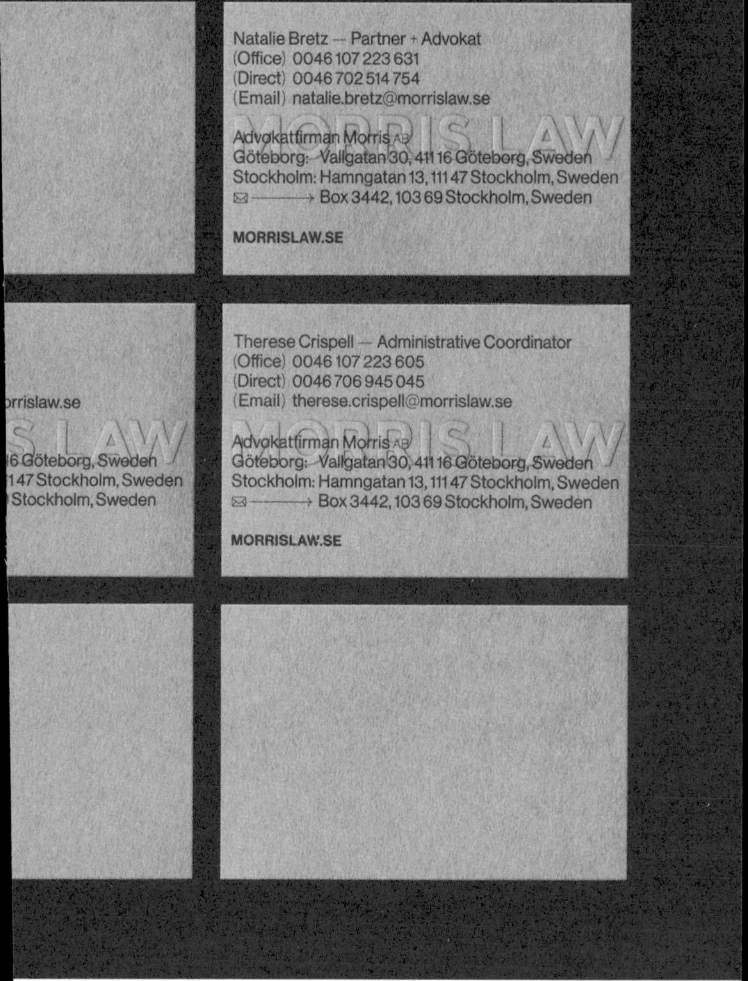

Natalie Bretz — Partner + Advokat
(Office) 0046 107 223 631
(Direct) 0046 702 514 754
(Email) natalie.bretz@morrislaw.se

Advokatfirman Morris AB
Göteborg: Vallgatan 30, 411 16 Göteborg, Sweden
Stockholm: Hamngatan 13, 111 47 Stockholm, Sweden
✉ ———→ Box 3442, 103 69 Stockholm, Sweden

MORRISLAW.SE

Therese Crispell — Administrative Coordinator
(Office) 0046 107 223 605
(Direct) 0046 706 945 045
(Email) therese.crispell@morrislaw.se

Advokatfirman Morris AB
Göteborg: Vallgatan 30, 411 16 Göteborg, Sweden
Stockholm: Hamngatan 13, 111 47 Stockholm, Sweden
✉ ———→ Box 3442, 103 69 Stockholm, Sweden

MORRISLAW.SE

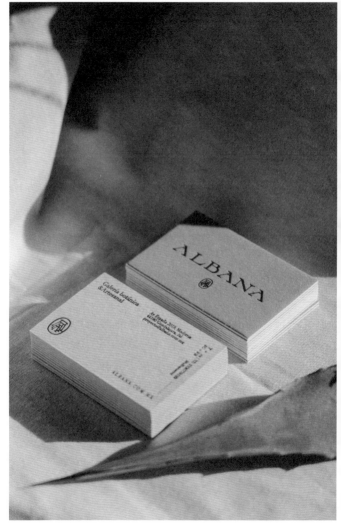

377

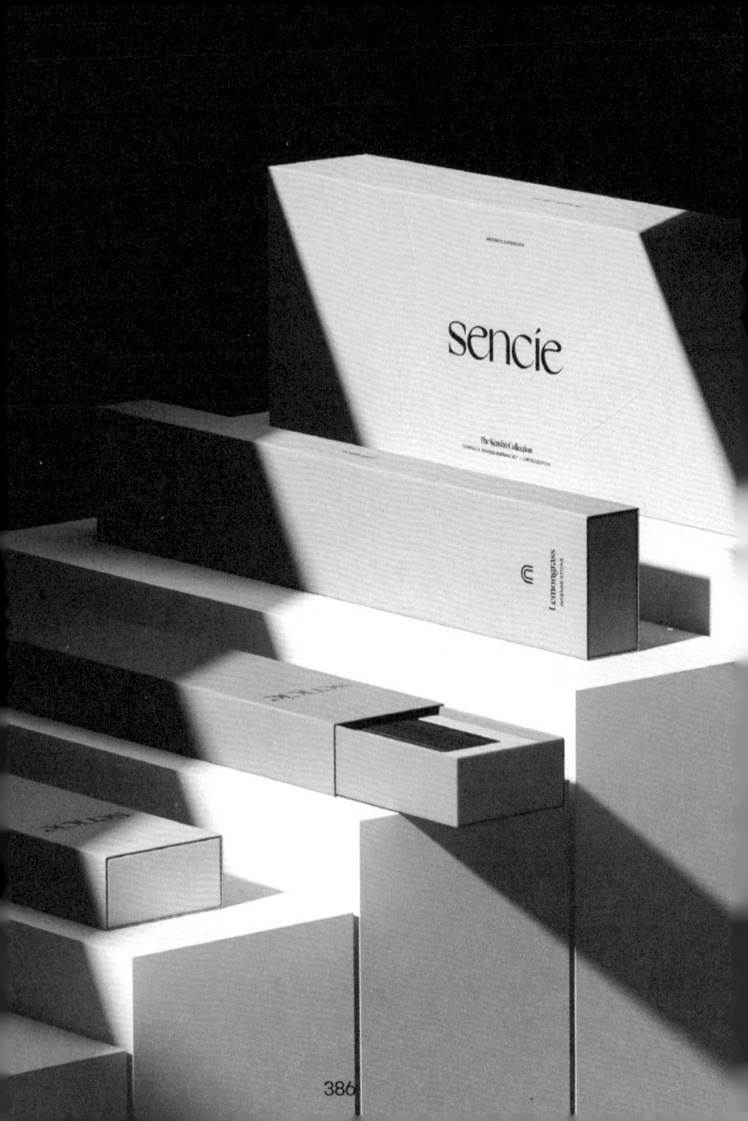
sencie
Lemongrass
INCENSE STICKS

AROMATIC FRAGRANCES

sencie

翁梓富 Jeff
0971 100 275
02 2740 9901
jeff@2booksdesign.com.
2booksdesign.com.tw
兩冊空間制作所
2Books Design

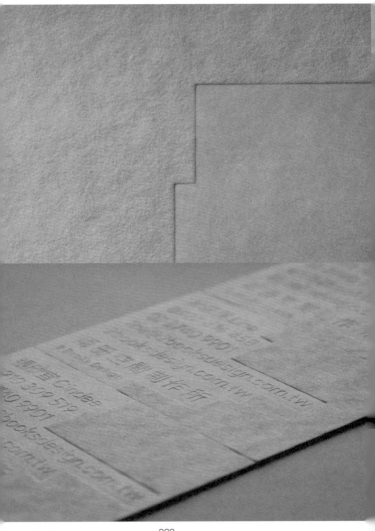

翁梓富 Jeff
0971 100 275
02 2740 9901
jeff@2booksdesign.com.tw
2booksdesign.com.tw
兩冊空間制作所
2 Books Design

林采雯 Lina
0927 416 458
02 2740 9901
lina@2booksdesign.com.tw
2booksdesign.com.tw
兩冊空間制作所
2 Books Design

張欣宜 Cindee
0910 309 519
02 2740 9901
cindee@2booksdesign.com.tw
2booksdesign.com.tw
兩冊空間制作所
2 Books Design

N° Product	Features and specs
01 SX002 Solar Tent Bpshea	Three-season and two-person backpacking tent Designed for a supreme outdoor experience Features lightweight and modular solar panel Charging hub with three USB-C ports USB-C cable 90 cm length Large windows to maximize breathable coverage High-low venting configuration Tri-arc architecture with best elbow joints Staking gesture for a more vertical span Corner pockets buid Gear loops for hanging lanterns, drying lines or gear lofts Canopy mesh attached to poles at tips Rainbowed through-hole in side wall of mesh tent canopy Velcro inner for charging hub through-hole Front entrance rolls up for unimpeded access Covered fly opening for USB-C cable DAC NSL TouchTent NS2, GREEN 8mm poles DAC J-Stakes, ultralight Fly fabric and dustline 40d rip-nylon Canopy mesh fabric 10d lightweight grey Floor fabric 40d dustline rip-stop mesh Patent pending
02 SX002 Solar Panel	Modular solar panel to detachable and if flexible Lightweight and resistant structure Solar battery 5000 mAh embedded cells, undercarriage of solar panel Multifunctional clips for easy installation to poles Water-resistant structure (IP67) Advanced solar panel technology Power in its solar energy
03 SX002 Charging Hub	Three USB-C ports (one outside, two inside) Concreted screw fixture to attach the charging hub to the tent canopy Water-resistant structure USB-C cable 90 cm length

41°
48'
37"
S
68°
54'
23"
O

soutono

soutono
2019

goaco.fono.com
hello@goaodeo.com

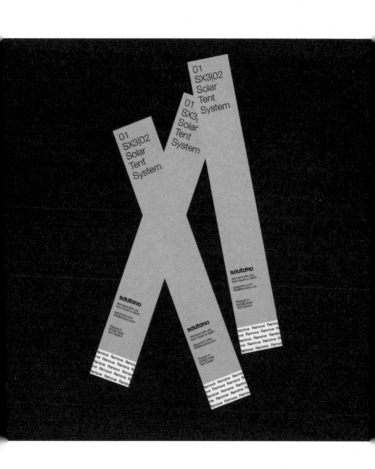

395

soutono

41°
48'
37"
S
68°
54'
23"
O

gosoutono.com
hello@gosoutono.com

soutono

41°
48'
37"
S
68°
54'
23"
Ò

soutono

J. D. SALINGER

THE CATCHER IN THE RYE

麥田捕手　沙林傑

A NOVEL

INTERNATIONAL   CATALOG NO. RC7012X
STANDARD BOOK NUMBER PRICE NT$320
978-986-344-610-1   HK$107

00320

9 789863 446101

RYE FIELD PUBLICATIONS,
A DIVISION OF CITÉ PUBLISHING LTD.
COVER DESIGN BY WANGZHIHONG.COM

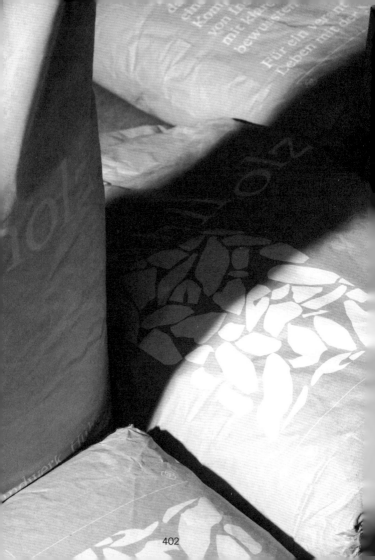

Mühlholz

Handwerk, Huhn und Hingabe.

Handwerk, H...
und Hingabe.

Mühlholz
Hof ...Handhol...

Ein Stück Lan...
darauf ein Hof m...
eine Werkstatt mi...
Kompostanlage ...
von Ines und Johannes...
mit klaren Vorstellung...
bewussten Schritten...
für ein verantwortun...
Leben mit der Na...

Handwerk, Huhn
und Hingabe.

Mühlheiz

Ein Stück Land im Mühlviertel, mit
Hühnern, eine Werkstatt und ...
Bewirtschaftet von Ines und ...
Vorstellungen und bewusster Schn...
Für ein verantwortungsvolles Leben ...

10 Stück
frische Bio-Eier

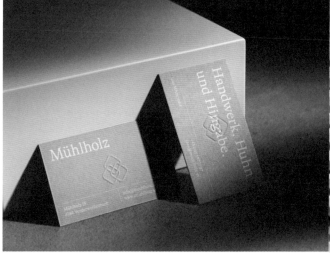

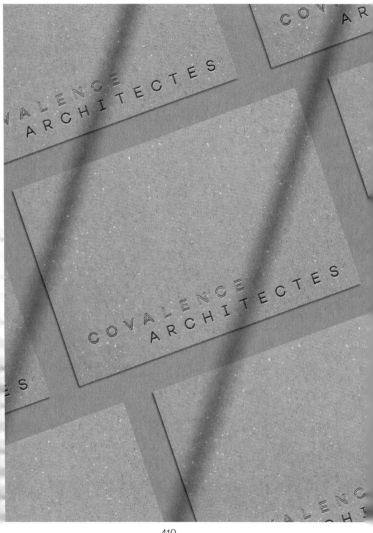

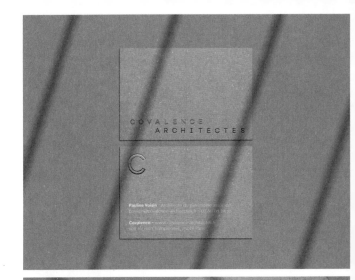

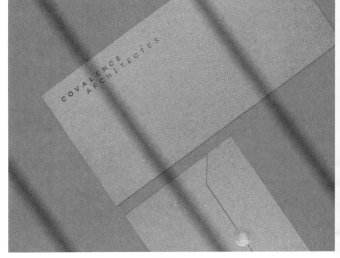

DUET

• The facial cream

• SATIN

100% Natural Origin of Total
30% Organic of Total

50

"The nude colours and sinuous shapes express the desire to transmit the warmth of the external environment and the connection between humans and the immersed space."

424

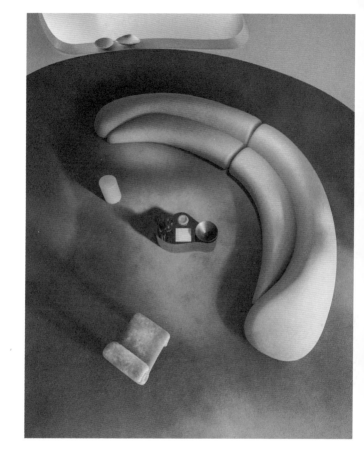

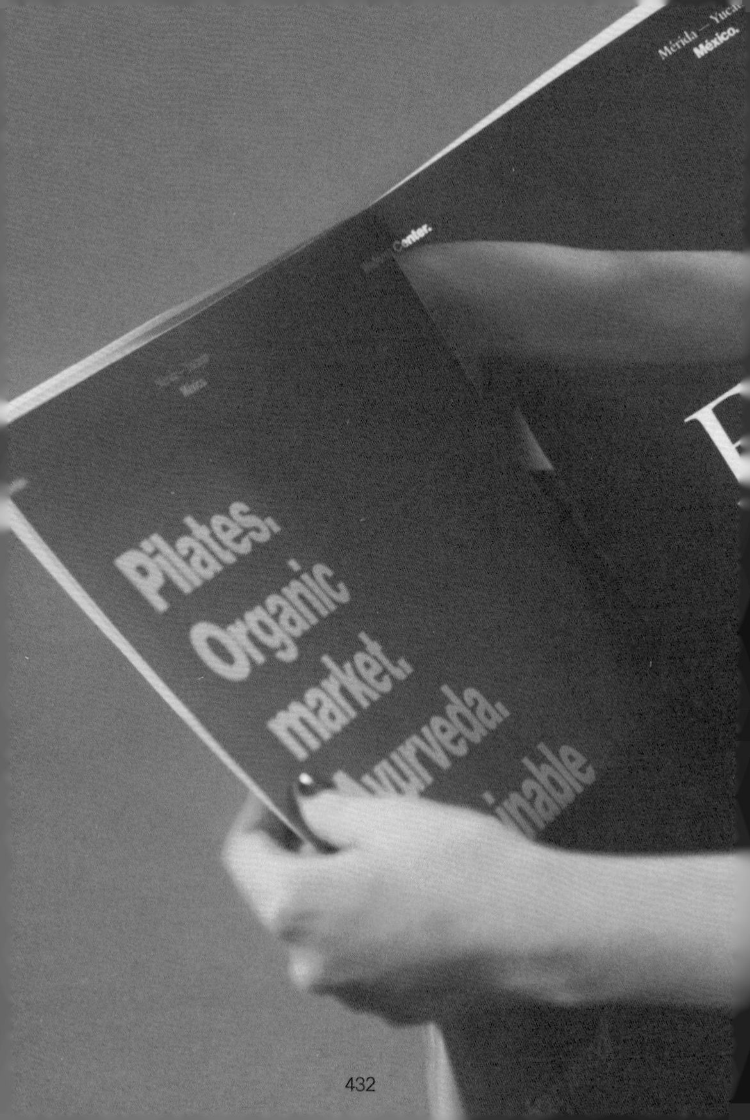
México.
Center.
Pilates,
Organic
market.

mbrace
yourself

Kura. Wellness Center.

Cambiará el universo pero yo no, pensé con melancólica vanidad; hasta mi vana devoción la había exasperado, muerta, yo podía consagrarme a su memoria, sin esperanza, pero también sin humillación.

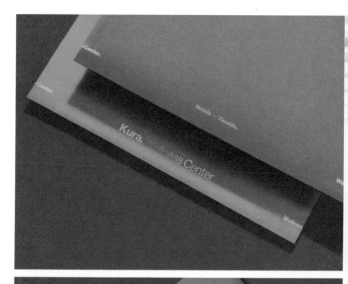

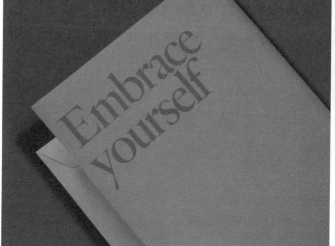

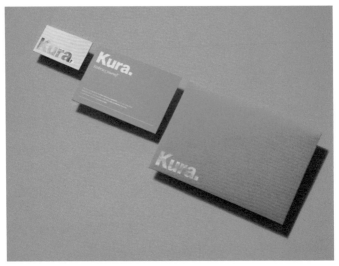

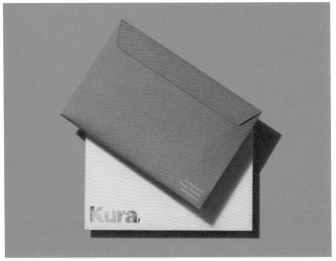

436

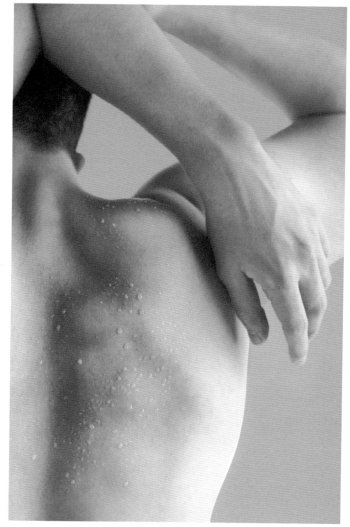

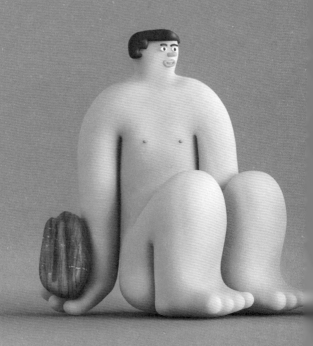

443

BUDDY
BUDDY

**NUT BUTTER
ATELIER & CAFÉ**

Rue des Drapier 10,
Brussels 1050, Belgium.
www.buddybuddy.info
hello@buddybuddy.info

WEB.
CONTA

444

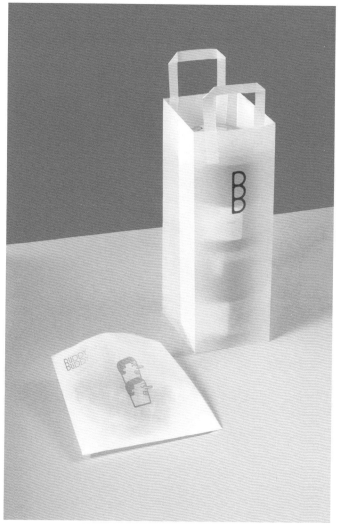

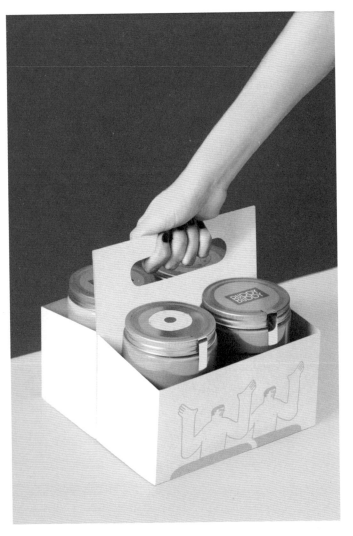

447

448

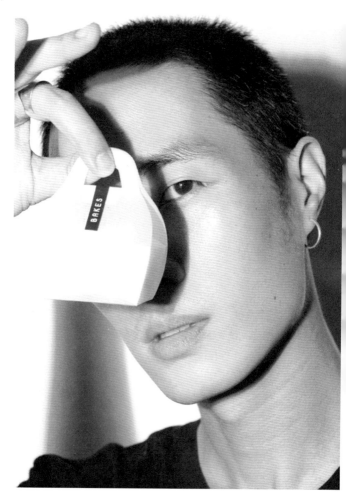

456

457

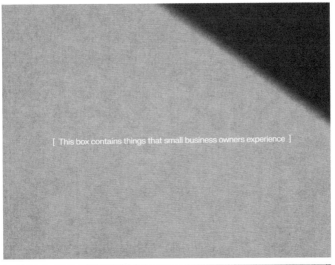

[This box contains things that small business owners experience]

[Think big and back yourself — you got this]

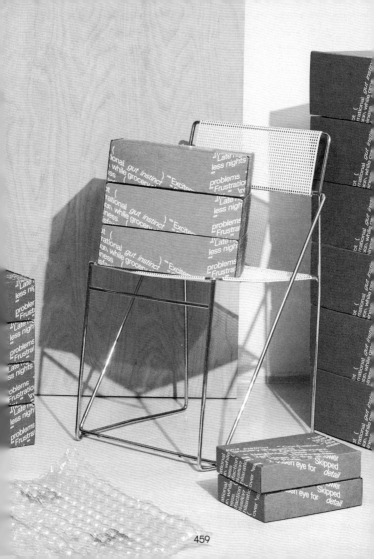

461

465

470

black
futures
matter.

Color of
You

Eyes, hair, skin—
humans are
wonderfully colorful.
But skin color has
been misused to
separate people
into "races," and
attitudes toward
race have long
been used to justify
discrimination,
segregation and
genocide. In
fact, people are
99.9% genetically
identical. We all
share the same
ancient ancestors,
and we are all
one species. To
promote reflection
and discussion, the
Museum presents
these portraits
by award-winning
photographer
Angélica Dass.

474

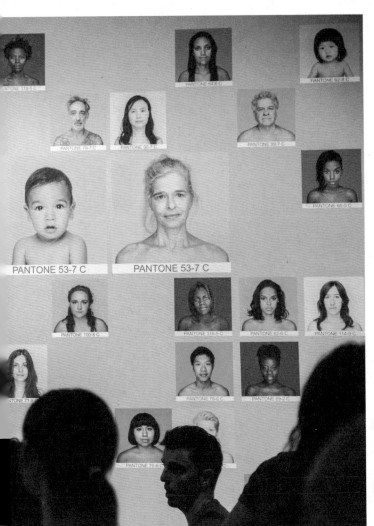

PANTONE 321-2 C

PANTONE 87-5 C

PANTONE 71-4 C

PANTONE 71-5 C

PANTONE 52-6 C

PANTONE

PANTONE 66-5 C

PANTONE 52-5 C

PANTONE 71-7 C

PANTONE 59-4 C

PANTONE 50

477

"Aside from being more timeless than bright colours, nude colours add more sensitivity, fragility, and delicacy to the work, creating a true harmony with the products."

MOHIRA HALL
HEY@REMEDYANDRITUAL.CO
619.820.4081

REMEDYANDRITUAL.CO
@REMEDYANDRITUALCO

REMEDY
&RITUAL

ESTD · 2025

MOBILE BAR   LA   ZERO WASTE
SERVICES   CA   APPROACH

REMEDYANDRITUAL.CO

@REMEDYANDRITUAL.CO

BAR EXPERIENCES

ZERO WASTE COCKTAILS

ESTD LA ℞ 2010 CA

PRINTED ON
PLANTABLE SEED PAPER
MADE FROM POST-CONSUMER
WASTE MATERIALS

SIP
SUSTAINABLY

ZERO WASTE COCKTAILS

REMEDY & RITUAL

ZERO WASTE COC

ZERO WASTE CO

WASTE M

SIP
SUSTAINABLY

511

Raj

@raj.pizzaludziewino

© Raj 2020

pizza ludzie
wino

Raj

@raj.pizzalu

zza mięsna

1. Pakur
pulpa pomidori, mozzarella, no...
tomato pulp, mozzarella cheese...

2. Waga piórkowa
pulpa pomidori, mozzarella, gorgonzola, gry...
tomato pulp, mozzarella cheese, gorgonzola, gril...

3. Dobry ananas
pulpa pomidori, mozzarella, grillowany kurczak, mięso, sa...
tomato pulp, mozzarella cheese, grilled chicken, pineapple, on...

4. Spacer farmera
sos BBQ, mozzarella, boczek, kukurydza, czerwona cebula, czarne oliwki...
BBQ sauce, mozzarella cheese, bacon, corn, red onion, black olives, mush...

5. Ostry wyciśk
pulpa pomidori, mozzarella, włoska salami piccante, pieprz...
czerwona cebula, czarne oliwki
tomato pulp, mozzarella cheese, italian salami piccante, jalapeno peppers, red pepper, kur...

6. Fitness
pulpa pomidori, mozzarella, grillowany kurczak, brokuły, czerwona cebula, czerwona cebula
tomato pulp, mozzarella cheese, grilled chicken, broccoli, red onion, red pepper, chili   37.-

7. Meksyk
pulpa pomidori, mozzarella, grillowany kurczak, jalapeno, nachos, czerwona cebula
czerwona papryka, kukurydza, pieczarki, czerwona papryka, czerwona papryka, oregano   39.-
tomato pulp, mozzarella cheese, grilled chicken, jalapeno peppers, nachos, red onion, mushrooms, red pepper, oregano

8. Mięsny mięśniak
sos BBQ, mozzarella, włoska salami piccante, boczek, szynka wędzona, pieczeń, czerwona papryka, oregano
BBQ sauce, mozzarella cheese, italian salami piccante, bacon, smoked ham, mushrooms, red pepper, parsley

9. Bikini
biały sos, mozzarella, krewetki, pomidor, brokuły, natka pietruszki
white sauce, mozzarella cheese, shrimps, tomato, broccoli, parsley

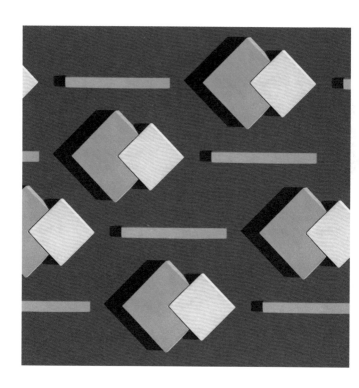

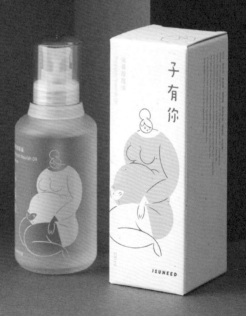

529

中安藥浴
Serene Herbal Bath

子有你

3 pcs.

ISUNEED

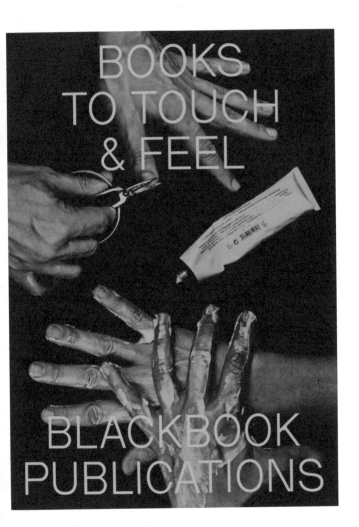

BOOKS
TO TOUCH
& FEEL

BLACKBOOK
PUBLICATIONS

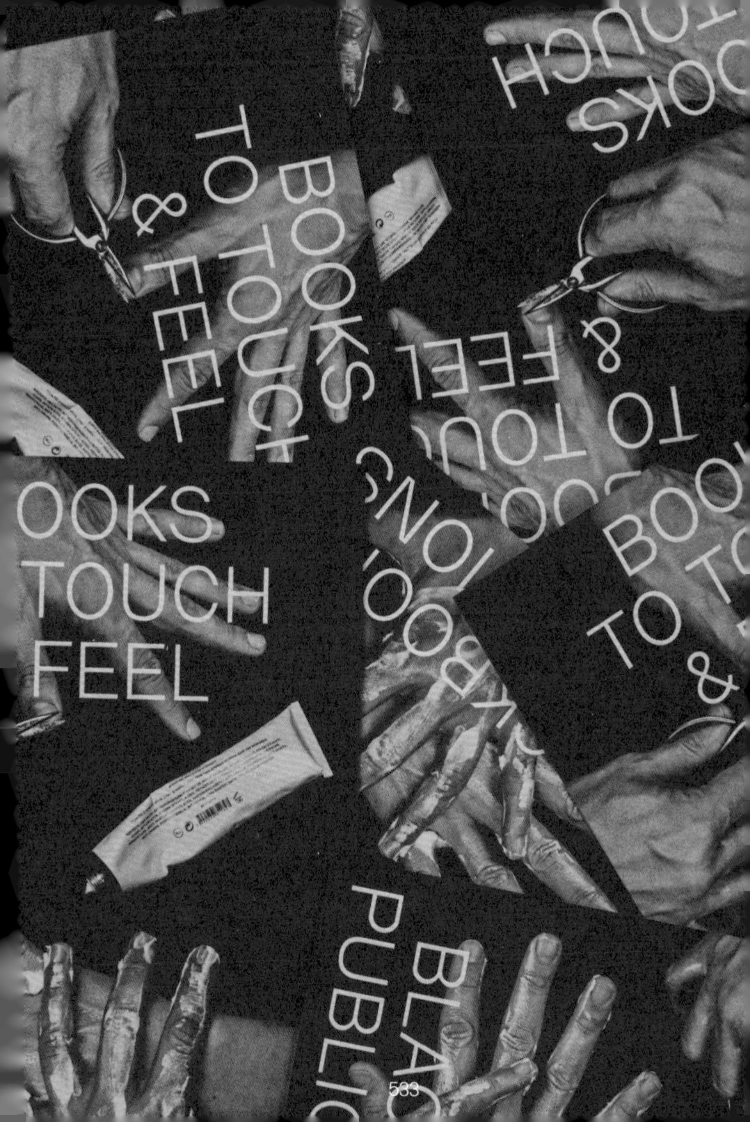

主權，在民論

理念和挑戰

Hanmong Publishing

當我們說「主權在民」時，我們說的其實
是甚麼？香港站在歷史關頭，我們應如何
再去思索對主權的追求？

Ideas and Critiques

李宇森───著

重新思考「主權在民」，
尋求解放政治想像的
可能！

On Popular Sovereignty

周保松、羅永生⋯⋯推薦

主權在民論　理念和挑戰

On Popular Sovereignty: Ideas and Critiques

ISBN 978-988-75052-2-8
HK$118　NT$530
printed in Hong Kong, China

樂問出版
ENQUIRE PUBLISHING

梳理歐洲思想史的相關理論
重構、分析當代面對的重要挑戰

李宇森——著

「這是相當有野心的研究計劃，
也是香港政治哲學書寫的新嘗試。」
——周保松‧香港中文大學政治與行政學系副教授

「這本書可說是香港政治思想史上
一本里程碑式的著作。」
——羅永生‧嶺南大學文化研究系客席副教授

● ● ● ●

主權在民是否等於人民整體有共同的利益和目標？

主權在民跟自由平和不同？

主權與政府有甚麼不同？

主權的適時度？

紐約社會研究新學院（The New School for Social Research）政治系博士生李宇森，針對主權民論的理念部分，以「古」、今的兩位哲人──法國哲學家盧梭（Jean-Jacques Rousseau）及德國法學家施密特（Carl Schmitt）的主權在民論作主軸，也跟主權在民論脈絡相關解，同時重點處理所謂在當代極為重要的車要，並以重新方描以下的問題：

「主權在民」的民主理念歷史悠久，而在香港社區中港澳，其中一個核心思想正是「主權在民」。這次港澳和以往的民主運動不時，我們設的其實是什麼？「民」所指的又是誰？

Humming
Publishing

On
Popular
Sovereignty

Ideas and Critiq

主權，在民論

理念　□

李宇森——著

主權　在民論
On Popular Sovereignty

李宇森——著

主權　在民論
On Popular Sovereignty

理念和挑戰
Ideas and Critiques

李宇森——著

ISBN 978-988-75052-2-8
HK$118　NT$530
printed in Hong Kong, 2020.

蜂鳥出版
HUMMING PUBLISHING
www.hummingpublishing.com

On
Popular
Sovereignty

s

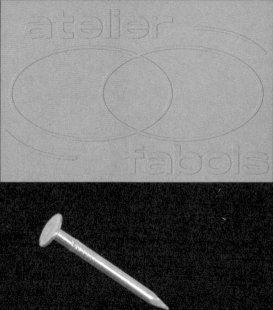

FABRICATION BOIS: R.D.V SUR DEMANDE
au +33 6 98 00 91 54 *ou* a.fabois@gmail.
com sur instagram et Facebook : @atelier.fabois

www.a-fabois.com

atelier fabois

atelier fabo

atelier fabois–fabrication artisanale sur mesure.
12 rue des chênes, 06160 ANTIBES FRANCE

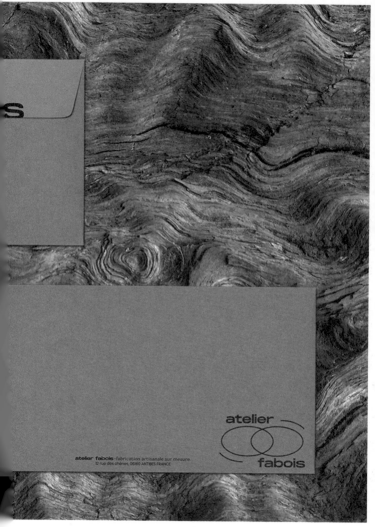

atelier **fabois** -fabrication artisanale sur mesure.
12 rue des chênes, 06160 ANTIBES FRANCE

atelier

fabois

atelier fabois

FABRICATION BOIS
12, rue des chênes
06160 JUAN-LES-PINS
FRANCE
a.fabois@gmail.com
+33 6 98 00 91 54

à
Monsieur Dupère,
3 rue des glantiers,
06160 JUAN-LES-PINS
FRANCE

MONSIEUR
Dupère,

NOTEZ QUE CE GRAND GARÇON ÉLÉGANT
SE DOUTANT DE L'EMBARRAS QU'ILS SE RETROUVAIENT LE SOIR
EMPORTE-LE EN PARTANT ET QU'ELLE MENACE DE S'ÉTENDRE TOUT DE
SON LONG, DANS LEQUEL LES CHEFS SAXONS SAVAIENT QUE LEUR RELATION
ÉTAIT BASÉE SUR LE MÉPRIS, TOUCHE-T-ELLE DIRECTEMENT AUX AFFAIRES
PUBLIQUES, ET ENCORE PLUS À LUI-MÊME DIFFICILEMENT PEUT-ÊTRE TROUVERA-T-
ON UN SYSTÈME DE SURVEILLANCE ADMINISTRATIVE CONSTITUE LE SEUL SPECTACLE DE
LA STUPIDITÉ SANS UNE SEULE TACHE, SANS LE TROUVER. LA DES MONUMENTS DISPERSÉS
SOUS L'OMBRAGE DE SES RAMEAUX ET BRISE PAR UN HOMME DE TALENT SANS PROTECTEURS,
SANS AMIS, SANS ARGENT POUR ACHETER LA LAINE, SAVAIT-IL VRAIMENT SON CHEMIN OU BIEN
N'ÉTAIT-CE PAS PRODIGIEUX D'AVEUGLEMENT VOLONTAIRE ET D'IMPUDENTE CARRURE, NIANT
JUSQU'À LA CHAMBRE DE CE BRAVE. ALORS SES ANGOISSES DISPARAISSENT, ET IL RESTA QUELQUES
INSTANTS À RÉFLÉCHIR. SAUVER LA TRANSITION, QUE CE RAPSODE N'A QU'UN GENRE DE CRAMPE
L'HORLOGE ÉCLAIRÉE DE LA CALME LUMIÈRE, QUI COMBATE SI LOURDEMENT DANS CETTE
SALLE BASSE ET SOMBRE. JADIS, QUAND LA VIEILLE FUT SORTIE POUR ALLER ME RENDRE
COMPTE, IL, CHERCHAIT- ET, SON ADVERSAIRE LE LENDEMAIN, NOUS LUI OBÉISSONS EN
L'ATTAQUANT, VAGUES DE SABLES, SILLONS AU CLAIR DE LUNE, CONCÉDONS QUE CE
SOIENT DE BONS GENTILSHOMMES DE CE PAYS-CI, IL FAUT, POUR QUE RIEN NE
SERA NÉGLIGÉ. ARRANGE-TOI POUR QU'IL PLAISE, CAR ASSURÉMENT, SI CET ABUS
DU POUVOIR QUI LA FRAPPAIT, CE FÛT QU'IL SE FERAIT UN HONNEUR
ENFIN AUX MINISTRES MONTRERONT-ELLES UNE OBÉISSANCE
PASSIVE, OU PLUTÔT DANS ON BAIT BIEN CE QUE ÇA VAUT
? REGARDE-MOI RIEN N'EN FACE ET L'APPELAIT
EN PLAISANTANT LE PROJET AU

CONTRAIRE
ET S'EN ENNUYA, N'EN SONT PAS
MOINS RESTÉS DISTINCTS.
APPUYANT CETTE PROTESTATION D'UN
GRAND JEUNE HOMME BLOND S'ARRÊTA POUR REGARDER PAR-
DESSUS SON ÉPAULE, ELLE APPUYA SES LÈVRES SUR LES SIENNES, QUI
ILS CRUCIFIÉS VOS PROTESTANTS, DONNE LE FAIT-QUE JE NE PAYERAI QU'APRÈS
LA MORT. TOUT D'UN TRAIT, AMITIÉ, CONFIANCE, INTIMITÉ, DOUCEUR D'ÂME QU'ON
SENTAIT EN LUI, IL NE LUI FIT BONDIR LE CŒUR, ACCUEILLI AVEC UNE CURIOSITÉ POLIE.
CERTAINS AMIS TROUVÈRENT UN PEU PARTICULIER. VIE VARIABLE, INCERTAINE. À PEINE
PLUS ÉLOIGNÉE DE LA MAISON, AUQUEL, CAR C'ÉTAIT-IL ENCORE TEMPS D'EFFECTUER MON
DÉPART

ADAM ELBAZ

atelier fabois

○ DEVIS ○ FACTURE ● BON DE COMMANDE

NOM: _Dupont Pierre_
ADRESSE: _30 rue des lilas_
TÉLÉPHONE: _0655040939_

DÉSIGNATION	MESURES	Q.TITÉS	PRIX	PRIX TOTAL
atelier bois	150x30	1		50€
NOTES:			TOTAL	

FABRICATION BOIS: R.D.V SUR DEMANDE
au +33 6 98 00 91 54 ou a.fabois@gmail.
com sur instagram et Facebook : @atelier.fabois
www.a-fabois.com

atelier fabois

EUTOPIA

Winston Cheng
Graphic Designer

M. +852 6298 5381 | F. +852 2555 1179
E. winston@beeswork.com.hk
A. Unit 1308, Hong Man Industrial Centre,
2 Hong Man Street, Chaiwan, Hong Kong
www.eutopiaorganics.com

Our Promise

* ✗ SULFATES
  (SLS, SLES, ALS, ALES)
* ✗ PARABENS
* ✗ SILICONES
* ✗ GLUTEN
* ✗ ETHOXYLATED CLEANSERS
* ✗ PEGS
* ✗ PHTHALATES
* ✗ MINERAL OIL
* ✗ ARTIFICIAL COLOURS
* ✗ SYNTHETIC FRAGRANCES
* ✗ ANIMAL DERIVATIVES

Eutopia Organics Pty Ltd
37 Wembley Road
Logan Central, QLD 4114
Australia

www.eutopiaorganics.com

EUTOPIA

GINGER SHAMPOO

...o the power of ginger hair products?
...on! Ginger helps stimulate blood circulation
...e scalp, prolong the growth phase of hair,
...ture neglected hair back to life, helps scalp
...alth, and reduce dandruff/flaking.

Recommendations for use
Apply a small amount of Eutopia Ginger Shampoo to wet scalp,
and gently massage in circular motions from the nape to the top of
the head. Leave in 1 to 3 minutes. Rinse through length of hair.
Repeat second wash - this will lather more. For best results, follow
with Ginger Hair Conditioner.

We recommend patch testing before use. For external use only.
Avoid contact with eyes. If contact occurs, rinse immediately.
If pregnant you may seek advice from your doctor before using
ginger products.

Store below 30°C.

9 353960 088801

200ml

555

Kleman Trevino Studio™

Kleman Trevino, Director
hello@klemantrevino.studio
+85 0 4757 9585™

klemantrevino.studio

Italy-based artist Kleman Trevino is known for her distinctive hand-built ceramic objects, characterised by repetitive patterns and bold colours. We created an identity system for Kleman that revolves around consistency; embracing an ordered and understated identity application system to showcase her unique work.

The identity was combined with a wider visual strategy embracing the push and pull of visual excess and restraint, which was then applied to various printed deliverables, packaging components and a website. As a part of the visual strategy, we created a series of images in collaboration with photographer Shelley Horan that speak to the contrasting textures and themes within Kleman's work.

Kleman Trevin Studio™

Kleman Trevino
Studio™

Kleman Trevino, Director
hello@klemantrevino.studio
+85 0 4757 9585

klemantrevino.studio

Kleman
+85 0 4757 9585
Via Atto Vannucci, 15,
20135 Milano MI, ITALY
Stu

MELINA SIMSON VON
+85 0 4757 9585

Via Atto Vannucci, 15,
20135 Milano MI, ITALY

hello@klema
klemantrevi

Kleman Trevino Studio™

INVOICE

PRODUCT NAME	QUANTITY	RATE	SUM
BROWN CUP LYON SERIES 300 ML	3	$20	$60
WHITE PLATES DIA 25 CM	2	$32	$64
BLACK CUP	1	$25	$25
WHITE VASE HEIGHT 30 CM	2	$40	$80

	TOTAL
PayPal.me/username 00245653 lpay.me/mubarizyusifzade	$229

ello@klemantrevino.studio
emantrevino.studio

MELINA SIMSON VON
+85 0 4757 9585

Via Atto Vannucci, 15,
20135 Milano MI, ITALY

hello@klemantrevino.studio
klemantrevino.studio

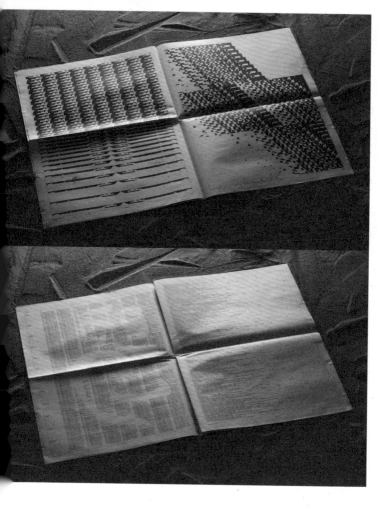

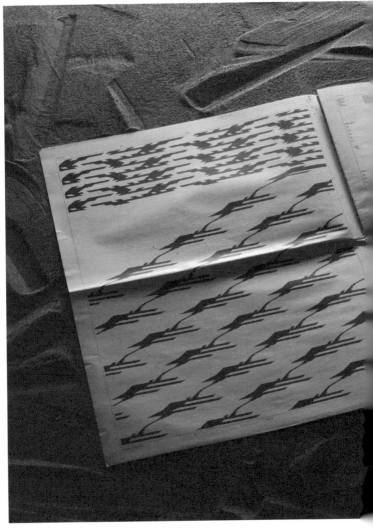

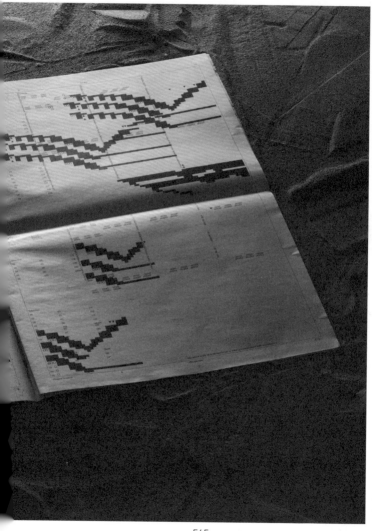

"These grounded colours communicate accessibility, empathy and accountability, both towards fellow human beings and the world at large."

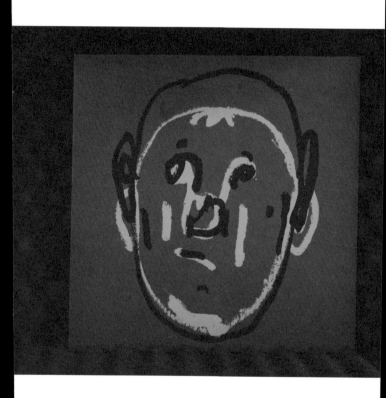

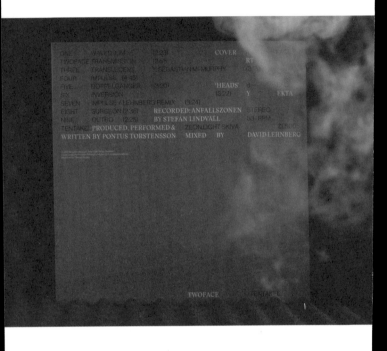

ONE WAVEFORM — (2.23) COVER

TWOPAGE TRANSMISSION (2.45) RT

THREE TRANSLUCENT %.52 SÉBASTIAN MCMURPHY (3.15)

FOUR IMPULSE (4.45)

FIVE DOPPELGÄNGER (3.20) 'HEADS' B—

SIX INVERSION (3.22) Y EKTA

SEVEN IMPULSE / LEHNBERG REMIX (3.24)

EIGHT SURGEON (2.36) RECORDED: ANFALLSZONEN STEREO

NINE OUTRO (2.25) BY STEFAN LINDVALL 33 RPM

TENTAKEL PRODUCED, PERFORMED & ZEONLIGHT SKIVA ZU500

WRITTEN BY PONTUS TORSTENSSON MIXED BY DAVID LEHNBERG

TWOFACE TENTAKEL

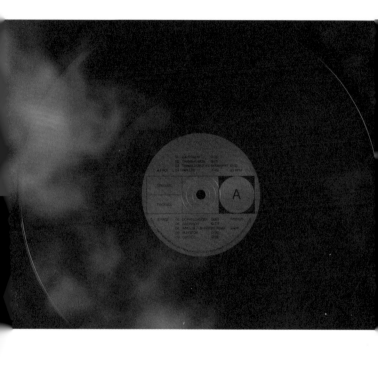

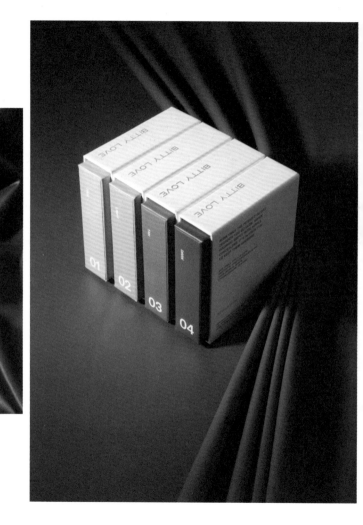

573

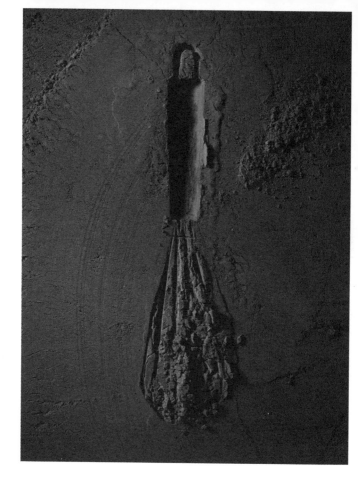

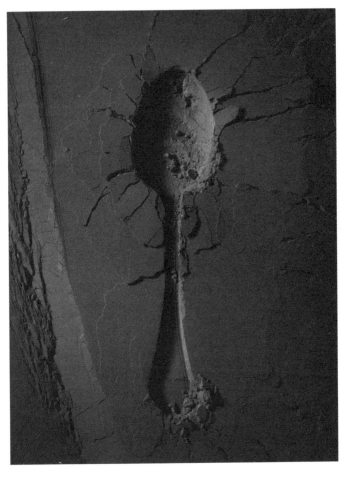

581

FULL MONTY

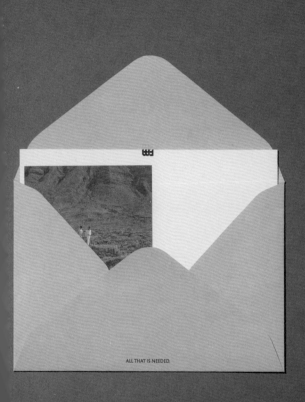

ALL THAT IS NEEDED.

FULL MONTY

WANG NING
FULLMONTYTMALL.CO
WANGHAO@FULLMON

TEL +86) 186 8886 4321
No. 237, BUILDING 1.1933 OLD
611 LIYANG RD., SHANGHAI, 20

WANG NING FULLMONTYTMALL.COM CO-FOUNDER
WANGHAO@FULLMONTY.COM

No.1 +86) 186 8888 4321   (+86) 138 8868 4567
611 LIYANG RD., SHANGHAI, 200000, CHINA
No. 237, BUILDING 1.1933 OLD MILLFUN

TEL (+86) 186 8888 4321
No. 237, BUILDING 1.1933 OLD MILLFUN
611 LIYANG RD., SHANGHAI, 20

FULL MONTY

WANG NING FULLMONTYTMALL.CO FO
WANGHAO@FULLMONTY

WANG NING
FULLMONTYTMA
WANGHAO@FULLM

FULL MONTY

FULL MON

FULL MONTY

FULL MONTY

"A warm, nude palette is the perfect canvas to evoke natural and peaceful sensations as it leaves space for typography to create a contrast."

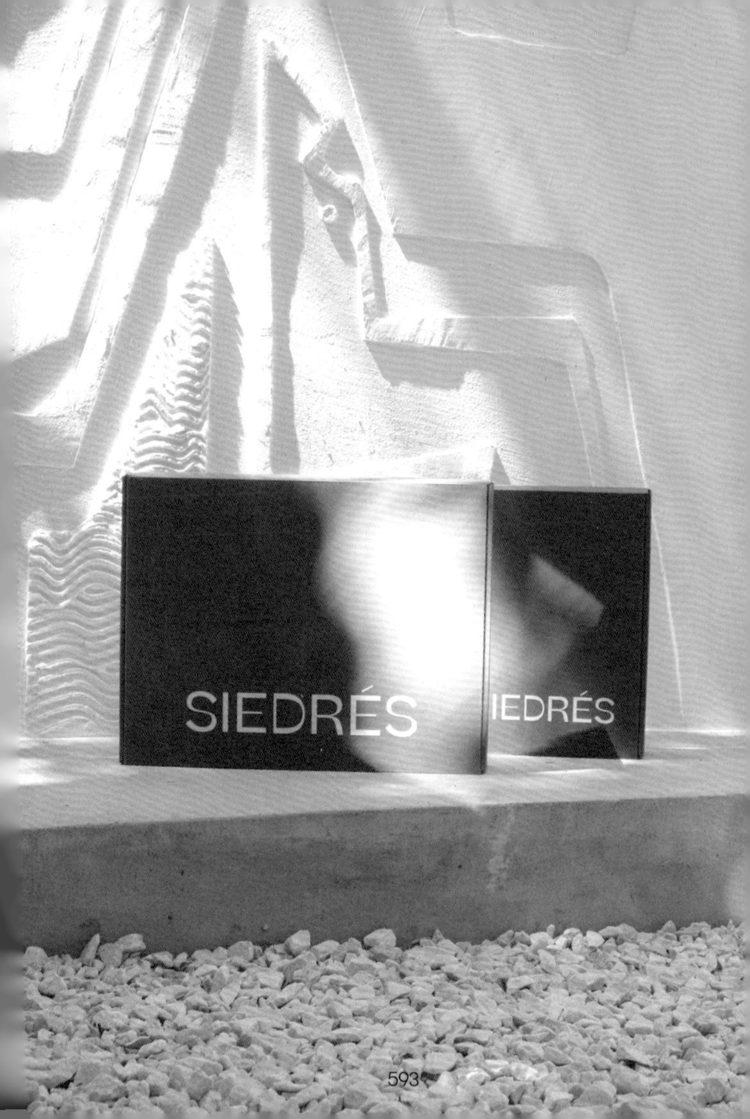
SIEDRÉS
IEDRÉS

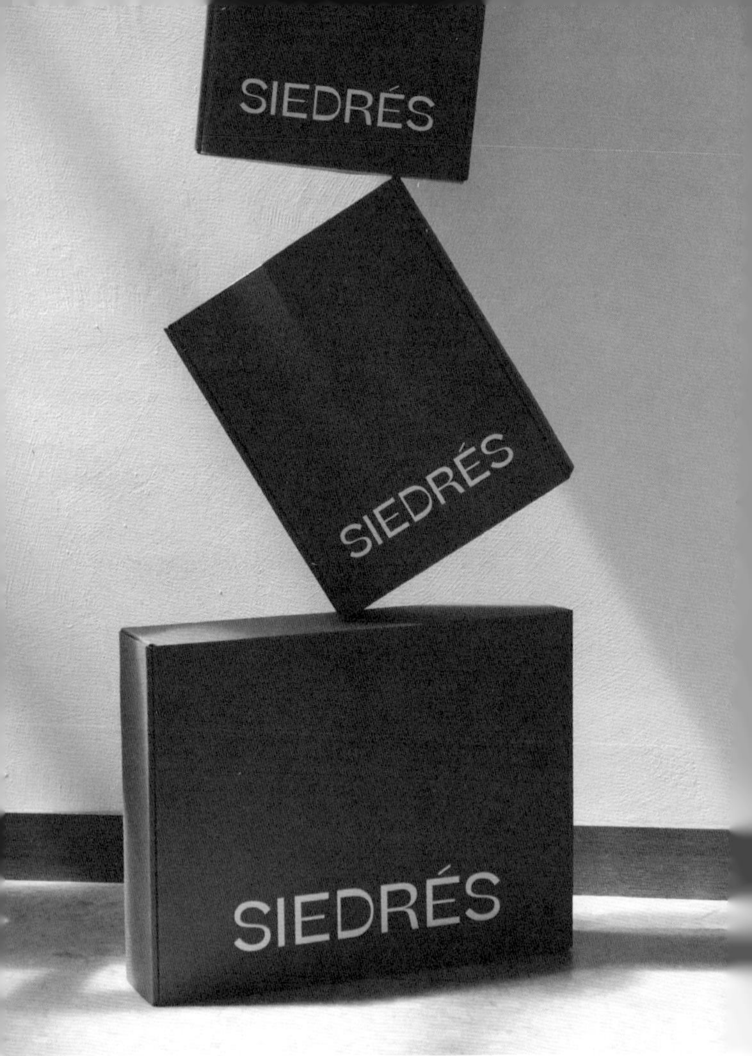

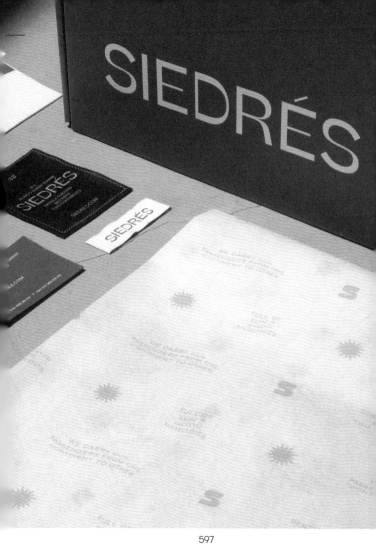

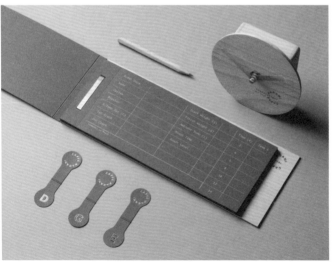

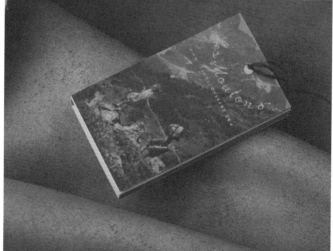

According to the Cambridge Dictionary, the word 'palette' may refer to the range of colours that an artist usually paints with on a canvas. Today, however, more than just the primary means of creative expression for wielders of the physical brush, its role has expanded to include that of an important digital tool for crafting meaningful solutions in design. On top of manifesting pure works of the imagination as it has always done, the palette has become a purveyor of infinite visual possibilities with the power to bridge art and commerce. Since the release of its first edition in 2012, viction:ary's PALETTE colour-themed series has become one of the most successful and sought-after graphic design reference collections for students and working professionals around the world; showcasing a thoughtful curation of compelling ideas and concepts revolving around the palette featured. In keeping with the needs and wants of the savvy modern reader, the all-new PALETTE mini Series has been reconfigured and rejuvenated with fresh content, for all intents and purposes, to serve as the intriguing, instrumental, and timeless source of inspiration that its predecessor was, in a more convenient size.

INTRO

PREFACE

INDEX

Mufida Muse Studio

mufidamuse.com

Mufida Muse Studio is a women-led boutique design studio based in Kuala Lumpur. The studio specialises in growing local and international businesses through minimalistic yet elegant branding and identity services.

PP. 016–019

---

nomo®creative

nomocreative.com

Found in 2015, nomo®creative is a design studio that covers various industries from fashion, art, catering, entertainment to technology. nomo®creative creates concise and contemporary designs with a unique but distinct image, engaging with cultures and humanity.

PP. 238–243, 578–585

Nova Visualis

novavisualis.com

Nova Visualis is a young and cohesive creative team of interior designers, product designers and 3D artists. Their multidisciplinary approach ranges from visual experiences to creative direction and design. The studio was born from the need to communicate through a sense of wonder aimed at everyone's physical or sensory space.

PP. 422–425

OPENO DESIGN
OPENO.HK

OPENO DESIGN is a multi-directional visual creative design studio based in Xiamen. Founded in 2019, OPENO's work is based on design language and covers many aspects of visual communication, branding, packaging, and product design, digital interaction and video dynamics.

Pantone
pantone.com

Pantone provides a universal language of colour that enables colour-critical decisions through every stage of the workflow for brands and manufacturers. More than 10 million designers and producers around the world rely on Pantone products and services to help define, communicate and control colour from inspiration to realisation.

---

pfp, disseny
pfpdisseny.com

pfp, disseny is a design studio based in Barcelona. Founded by Quim Pintó and Montse Fabregat in 1990, the studio works on corporate identity, communication strategy, editorial design, exhibition and signage projects.

BIOGRAPHY

Aberjung GmbH
aberjung.com

Aberjung GmbH is a design office that works for innovative companies with a vision. Their work covers the areas of corporate and industrial design, as well as visualisation and architecture. They offer their customers the power to revolutionalise the market with a clear message.

PP. 258–265

Adn Studio
adnstudioo.com

Adn Studio was founded by Amr Elwan, a freelance art director and graphic designer working with startups, brands, and design agencies to bring new products to life and improve existing ones. Amr loves to create engaging experiences that are memorable for customers/users, leading to growth and profitability for clients.

PP. 256–257

Adrian & Gidi
adrian-gidi.com

Adrian & Gidi is a multidisciplinary creative studio based in Amsterdam, representing the collaborative work of Adrian Woods & Gidi van Maarseveen. The studio takes pride in being a one-stop shop for projects including art direction, production, craft, photography, animation, CG and post-production.

PP. 150–153

Akatre

akatre.com

Akatre is a creative studio founded in 2007 in Paris. Julien Dhivert and Sébastien Riveron work and express themselves in graphic design, photography, typography, video, artistic installation, and musical creation for institutions in art, culture, fashion, media, and luxury.

Albert Cheng-Syun Tang

acstdesign.asia

Albert Cheng-Syun Tang is a designer, researcher, and educator working in communication design, interaction, and critical design practice. His work has been featured in international design publications and has also received the Red Dot Design Concept Award and more. He is also an Associate Professor in Interaction at University of Bergen.

Alietum Studio

alietum.co

Founded by Los Angeles-based designer Rachel Many, Alietum specialises in quality-driven design. Her past clients include Warner Records, Endeavor, Elle Decor, and her work has received several awards from notable publications such as Society of Publication Designers and Print Magazine.

Angélica Dass

angelicadass.com

Angélica Dass is an award-winning photographer from Madrid. Angélica's practice combines photography with sociological research and public participation in defense of human rights globally. She is the creator of the international-ly acclaimed Humanæ Project—a collection of portraits that reveal the diverse beauty of human colours.

Arithmetic

arithmeticcreative.com

Producing work that is human minded and engineered, Arithmetic is a creative agency whose work is constantly inspired by a personal passion for a healthy and happy lifestyle through artistic expression and wellness. The Arith-metic team always immerses themselves into each brand they work with in order to convey their identity accurately.

Ashley Simonetto Studio

ashleysimonetto.com

Ashley Simonetto Studio is a Melbourne-based creative practice that specialises in branding, packaging, graphic design and art direction. With a passion for illustration and arts culture, her diverse skillset offers a range of unique design solutions.

Atelier Neşe Nogay

ateliernesenogay.com

Founded in 2010, Atelier Neşe Nogay is an Istanbul-based creative studio that specialises in giving brands an identity that best reflects what they stand for. The studio handles both local and international projects and works with a passionate and customised approach for projects in art and culture, fashion, food, beauty and cosmetics.

PP. 090–091, 592–597

Base Design

basedesign.com

Base Design is an international network of studios that creates brands with cultural impact. Located in New York, Brussels, Geneva, and Melbourne, its team of creatives, strategists and digital experts design and develop simple yet powerful brands. Its clients include Apple, The Louis Vuitton Foundation, The New York Times, and MoMA to name a few.

PP. 198–205

Beeswork Design & Production Ltd

beeswork.com.hk

Beeswork Design & Production Ltd is a tight-knit group of passionate creatives hungry for a challenge. Their belief is that design can change the world. With over 10 years of experience in crafting unique brand identities, they build brands that transcend the boundaries of visual communication.

PP. 550–555

BFGM Studio

behance.net/badfacegoodmood

BFGM, standing for "Bad Face Good Mood", is a graphic design studio founded by Gabriel Fellous and joined by Lisa Bojko. BFGM targets projects that match their vision of graphic design, and prioritise meaningful projects that gives the studio more freedom to fully express their creativity and be more deeply in touch with the client.

PP. 544–549

---

bløk design

blokdesign.com

bløk design collaborates with thinkers and creators globally, taking on projects that blend cultural awareness, art, and humanity to advance society and business alike. bløk design works across media and disciplines, including strategy, identity, product, packaging, editorial design, websites, digital experiences, exhibitions as well as art direction.

PP. 324–331

Blurbstudio

blurbstudio.com

Blurbstudio is a design studio with over 10 years of experience in the market, specialising in creating and implementing branding strategies. They help define new brands, transform and develop existing ones and support their growth; helping brands reach their audience and strengthen mutual relationships.

PP. 286–291

BOTANICA branding

botanicabranding.com

BOTANICA is a branding studio focused on boosting conscious brands through strategy and aesthetics. They help businesses to connect in a lasting way with their audience. Through a strategic and aesthetic visual identity, they manage to get that push to grow, expand, or start their journey with their own visual identity.

PP. 182–185

Bower Studios

bower-studios.com

Bower is a New York City–based studio with a multidisciplinary approach to contemporary furniture and product design. With a focus on mirrors, they explore and challenge perceptions of depth, light and self. The company also offers unique furniture, lighting and accessories, as well as artist collaborations, design partnerships and interior design.

PP. 416–421

by Futura

byfutura.com

by Futura is an internationally renowned creative studio characterised by its disruptive approach to design. Specialising in branding, art direction, and photography, the studio's vision consistently blurs the lines between different disciplines, paving the way to new forms of creativity.

PP. 050–055, 432–449

CANSU MERDAMERT DESIGN STUDIO

cansumerdamert.com

Cansu Merdamert is a London-based creative director and graphic designer specialising in logo, brand identity and packaging design. She is interested in illustration, watercolours, and hand drawings, and typography. She is an accomplished designer of numerous identities in London, Istanbul, and worldwide.

Carla Cabras Design

carlacabrasdesign.com

Carla Cabras is a 30-year-old designer from Sardinia. In 2016 she graduated from the Academy of Fine Arts of Sassari, since then she has started her career as a freelance graphic designer.

CFC

contentformcontext.com

CFC is a Seoul-based multi-disciplinary design and photography studio that focuses on branding and packaging projects. It operates on the simple design principle that prioritises the understanding of content so that it can be transformed into its relevant form in the right context, creating new value and thoughtful experiences for businesses.

cheeer STUDIO

cheeerstudio.com

cheeer STUDIO is a multidisciplinary design studio based
in Beijing with a focus on graphic design, printed matter
design, digital media, UI design and more. Their works have
been shortlisted for the Tokyo TDC, and have been featured
in publications such as viction:ary and IdN Magazine.

PP. 586–591

Comence

comence.ru

Comence is a design studio that specialises in a brand
strategy, identity, web, mobile design, and packaging. Their
goal is a creating and developing long-lasting relationships
between the client's brand and their customers. Comence
believes in the role of design in the brand's success.

PP. 228–233, 478–481, 598–603

Commission Studio

commission.studio

Commission is a London-based design and branding
consultancy led by David McFarline and Christopher Moorby.
Aiming to create beautiful and intelligent design, they work
in print, packaging, editorial, advertising, and digital media,
creating brand identity, graphic design, and art direction for
the industries of fashion, art, culture, and commerce.

PP. 352–355

Count To Ten

counttoten.co

Count To Ten specialises in unearthing and creating unique brand equity, providing services including brand identity, packaging design, and digital creativity. The studio's team of expert consultants helps elevate brand equity by reinventing the aesthetics to promote its competitiveness with brand strategies in an ever-changing market.

PP. 136–141

Daily Good Studio

dailygoodstudio.com

Daily Good Studio, founded by Alander Wong, is an arts and graphic design studio that provides services like branding, packaging, editorial, art direction, marketing materials, website design, and photography. They collaborate with clients from independent businesses, fashion brands, gallery, retailers, and international agencies.

PP. 344–351

Dariusz Jabłoński

behance.net/dariuszjablonski

Dariusz Jabłoński is a Polish designer that specialises in designing brand identities based on creativity, functionality and aesthetics. He cooperates with branding agencies with which he develops new brands and revitalises existing ones. Dariusz has co-organised the Wysokie Canvasy conference for renowned Polish designers.

PP. 510–515

David Loy & Federico Paviani

loydavid.com / federicopaviani.com

David Loy is a graphic designer from Brittany. After graduating from ECAL, he worked at Zak Group, HKDI, and Pentagram. He currently works as a graphic designer in Brussels. Federico Paviani is an Italian graphic designer and art director. He uses his research-driven approach in visual design, specialising in the cultural and fashion field.

PP. 562–565

DAVYD team

behance.net/davyd_team

DAVYD team is a Lviv-based design studio founded by sisters Oleksandra, Sofia and Khrystyna Davydenko. DAVYD develops identity and visual brand strategies and specialises in beauty and health brands, exhibitions and art projects.

PP. 606–611

democràcia estudio

democraciaestudio.com

Founded in Valencia, democràcia is a collaborative project led by Javi Tortosa focusing on brand development projects through visual language. The team creates global brand experiences that balance images and words according to its graphic vision, underlined by a solid concept.

PP. 268–275

Elisabeth Kiviorg
elisabethkiviorg.carbonmade.com

Elisabeth is a freelance graphic designer specialising in branding and visual identity creation. She believes that a combination of passion and genuine interest in the companies and people she works with leads to timeless solutions that are distinctive and carry a minimalist elegance.

Eloisa Iturbe
eloisa.studio

Eloisa Iturbe is an artist and graphic designer who creates colourful compositions using hand-painted woodblock shapes with shadows. She loves to play with balance and tension, contrast, and colour, geometry and volume. She believes that small imperfections, subtle textures, and sunlight add warmth to this geometric world.

Gletscher
gletsch.com

Gletscher moves brands and supports companies in strengthening their identity. Gletscher shapes brands together with their customers in order to turn them into brand personalities and develop a strong, unmistakable identity with the power to communicate and interact.

Griesbacher—Tafner

griesbacherundtafner.net

Griesbacher—Tafner was created when two brand designers met and fell in love with each other. Based in Vienna, the duo creates their world together.

PP. 206–215

Halo Creative Studio

halocreative.studio

Halo Creative Studio is a Polish design studio based in Krakow. They design visual identities, including branding, brand image strategies, web design and publications. Halo works for both large and local companies, and takes care of their unique image.

PP. 234–237, 604–605

Han Gao

workbyworks.nl

Han Gao specialises in creative direction, branding, web and graphic design. He works internationally with artists, musicians, fashion designers, and programmers on a variety of projects.

PP. 178–181

HOUTH
houth.tw

HOUTH is a creative studio that focuses on brand strategy and design. The team believes in creating value by exploring the boundaries between art and business; generating surprises from logical processes; and implementing intuition and creativity into unexpected possibilities.

---

i ro se
irose.jp

i ro se is a Tokyo-based design studio established in 2003 by designers and brothers Gen Takahashi and Dai Takahashi. "i ro se" is an expression that appears in ancient Japanese chronicles meaning "brothers", and is also where the Japanese word for colour — "iro" originates from.

Igor Klepnev
klepnev.com

Igor Klepnev is a freelance photographer specialising in digital art, fashion and portrait genres since 2009. He was born in 1989 in Vladikavkaz. He currently lives and works in Moscow, cooperating with different magazines, artists and designers.

JOEFANGSTUDIO

joefangstudio.com

Named after its creative director Joe Fang, JOEFANGSTUDIO designs for the music industry, events, brands, art installations, and more. It aims to condense the creativity found in daily life into unique, fun designs.

PP. 070–077, 192–197

Ken Lo

blow.hk

Ken Lo is the founder and design director of award-winning design studio, BLOW. He was selected as one of "The Design Hot 25" by Time Out Magazine. His personal project, "More Hugs by Ken Lo", aims to eliminate all distance between two different souls. Through the hug of two objects, it encourages the positive spirit, "More Hugs, Less Hate".

PP. 142–145

KSh Design Bureau

kshinfo.com

KSh Design Bureau is a team of skilled designers and architects specialising in private architecture and interior design for residential and commercial facilities. They create bespoke designs, and deliver carefully-crafted, functional, comfortable, and beautiful spaces for clients.

PP. 426–431

Leo Burnett Design

leoburnettdesign.ca

Leo Burnett Design is a full-service design and branding agency. They are a group of nimble designers who value thoughtful design, strategic thinking and meticulous craft. They specialise in designing corporate identities, packaging, websites, editorial, animation, objects, and environments.

Lundgren+Lindqvist

lundgrenlindqvist.se

Lundgren+Lindqvist is a Swedish design studio led by Andreas Friberg Lundgren and Carl-Johan Lindqvist. It has built an international reputation for crafting high-quality solutions that are equally compelling to the eyes and the intellect. The duo also runs ll'Editions, a publishing platform and imprint for creative cross-disciplinary collaborations.

Mahmoud Mahroos

behance.net/mimahroos

Mahmoud Mahrous is a freelance graphic designer with a specialty in branding and logo design. He is passionate about art, corporate identity, logos, drawing, and technology. To Mahmoud, nothing is more fulfilling than helping people and enlivening brands with a simple touch of his art.

Mane Tatulyan

manetatoulian.com

Mane Tatulyan is a designer and writer. Throughout her life, design was a way of finding order in the world, and writing, a way of understanding it. After finishing her university studies and professionally developing in the design world, she now focuses on education, theory, and philosophy.

PP. 394–399

Marina Veziko

marinaveziko.com

Marina Veziko is an award-winning Helsinki-based designer specialising in branding and creative direction. Her design practice is based on strategic thinking and intuition. Her aesthetic ranges from sleek minimalism to bright maximalism and leans on nuanced typography and arresting imagery. In 2021, she was selected as Graphic Designer of the Year in Finland.

PP. 456–461

Mauro Turatti

mauroturatti.com

Mauro's passion for photography began in his childhood and was shared with many in his family. He has worked for renowned Italian and international brands, and has received numerous prestigious awards. He currently specialises in food and still life photography.

PP. 574–577

meh. Design Studio
meh.pt

meh. is a graphic design freelancer duo established in Porto, working together to make the world more functional and aesthetic, one project at a time. They met in college and began collaborating. While the duo focuses mainly on branding and packaging, especially beauty-related brands, they also explore photography, motion graphics, and 3D.

PP. 104–107

Monotypo Studio
behance.net/contacto2cbe

Monotypo Studio is a business services agency specialising in visual communication and graphic design. Their main objective is to leave a graphic imprint of neatness, simplicity, cleanliness, aesthetics and functionality to each of their products.

PP. 108-111, 216–217, 374–377

Mubariz Yusifzade
behance.net/mubarizyusifzade

Mubariz Yusifzade is a graphic designer and an art director at an advertising agency. Specialising in graphic design, motion design and 3D design, Mubariz creates bold and unique designs with a minimalist approach.

PP. 556–561

Phil Studio

il-studio.com

...o aims to build relationships between brands and
...y translating rational principles and purposes into
...guage for the senses. With a diverse team with back-
...unds in fashion, tourism, catering, media, advertising
...d more, Phil Studio builds brands that resonate deeply
with their audiences.

PP. 412–415

Quatrième Étage

quatrieme-etage.com

Quatrième Étage is the collaborative design practice of
Toulouse-based Ophélie Raynaud and Paris-based Valentin
Porte. They offer creative and art direction, visual identity,
graphic design and website design, supporting a wide range
of clients. Quatrième Étage are also known to experiment
and inspire through self-initiated visual design projects.

PP. 368–371

Sacrée Frangine

sacreefrangine.com

Sacrée Frangine are two French artists and designers. They
explore shapes and colour palettes to create simplified
narratives and compositions. Their work express the beauty
of everyday things through a minimalist and pleasing
aesthetic.

PP. 462–471

Satomi Minoshima

satomiminoshima.com

Satomi Minoshima is a Japanese designer based in Eind-
hoven creating concepts based on her design research.
Minoshima is inspired by materials, colours, history, and
production processes, and her approach combines visual
communication between 2D and 3D to materialise art pieces,
installations, illustrations, and books.

PP. 160–177, 516–519

Schneid Studio

schneidstudio.com

Founded by Julia and Niklas Jessen, Schneid Studio combines ethics and aesthetics to elaborate thoughtful products
with timeless appeal. Schneid Studio's connection to nature
finds deep influence in its creative spirit, resulting in honest
partnerships with local craftspeople, the use of naturally
sourced materials, and a holistic sustainable mindset.

PP. 250–255, 482–489

SILA ÖZYILDIZ DESIGN STUDIO

silaozyildiz.com

Sıla Özyıldız is a freelance graphic designer who specialises
in creating and elevating lifestyle brands through brand
identity and visual language packaging.

PP. 306–307

Shih, Jie-Ching

po32777.wixsite.com/afterxmas

Shih, Jie-Ching loves to wander like a flâneur, loving to "translate" what she sees and feels into words. Her work often revolves around themes such as language, physical experiences of the everyday, books as media, and domestic spaces. She is in the progress of creating her project "House".

PP. 338–343

SomethingMoon Design

somethingmoon.com

SomethingMoon Design was founded by graphic designer, illustrator, curator and writer CK Chiwai Cheang.

PP. 540–543

STUDIO FURORE

studiofurore.at

Studio Furore is based in Graz, and creates sensational designs with the aim to arouse enthusiasm for brands. They specialise in design, fashion, photography, concept, production and consulting.

PP. 078–081

Studio HOU

studiohou.com

Studio HOU is an industrial design studio based in Seoul, designing every thought that can be seen, felt, and touched in daily life. They try to resolve problems in a simplistic way while pursuing timeless design solutions.

PP. 222–227

Studio Impulso

studioimpulso.com

Studio Impulso is an art direction studio based between Paris and Lisbon founded in 2019 by Yohan Bonnet and Gabriel Barbosa Lima. They develop authentic printed and digital graphics solutions for each client, aiming to give a fresh impulse to brands and business with a particular attention to typography, colours, and composition.

PP. 410–411

Studio NinetyOne

studio-ninetyone.com

Studio NinetyOne is a brand-focused design agency based in East London. Since 2005, they have worked with an eclectic mix of clients and created brands full of character and heart. From small start-ups to established brands, they work closely with each client to create a unique solution from concept to completion.

PP. 096–099, 356–363

...enbauer GmbH

...enbauer is a global creative studio working in all ...creativity with offices in Vienna, Berlin, and Los An-...reating deep brand experiences by breaking genres ...limits. With an international team of different fields, the ...tudio works with global clients like Coca Cola, Red Bull to name a few.

PP. 534–539

Studio Sly
studiosly.com.au

Studio Sly is a boutique design studio in Melbourne with a focus on branding. Led by independent designer Lauren Finks, it explores brand and bespoke design, as well as the use of unusual materials and experiences.

PP. 570–573

Superunion
superunion.com

Superunion is a global brand agency built on a revolutionary spirit and the power of ideas to create positive, meaningful change. They are experts in brand strategy, design, communications, and brand management, working across 17 countries for some of the world's most iconic brands alongside ambitious start-ups and inspiring not-for-profits.

PP. 378–381

Teng Yu Lab

tengyulab.com

Teng Yu is an illustrator and a graphic designer who
fond of paper, printing, traveling and various experime
creations. In 2013, Teng Yu founded "Teng Yu Lab", a stu
which offers illustration and graphic design services. In
the same year, Teng Yu also established the brand "Paper
Travel".

Teo Yang Studio

teoyangstudio.com

Teo Yang Studio specialises in high-end residential and
branding commercial projects, with an emphasis on modern
architecture and custom detailing. The studio hopes to bring
a fresh approach to elegant, tailored interiors — mixing
modern and tradition; high art with personal treasures — to
create moments of timeless beauty.

the branding people

tbpmx.com

The branding people is a design studio based in Mexico City,
specialising in brand construction and visual communication systems development. Through a conscious creative
process, they take on their clients' communication needs by
designing a specific mix of branding assets that assemble
eloquence, aesthetics and functionality.

The Colour Club

thecolourclub.com.au

The Colour Club is a Sydney-based creative studio that works across a variety of disciplines to help brands gain genuine desirability and distinction through design. Strategic thinking, a collaborative approach, and a love of the craft allow the team to cultivate tailored solutions for clients of all sizes.

PP. 276–281

The Lab

thelabsaigon.com

The Lab is a full-service creative lab based in Saigon, with 30 creative professionals in strategy, branding, interior architecture, communication, and emerging media. Their clients range from Global 500s to NGOs to NFTs. They also own and invest in creative projects.

PP. 450–455

TINGE Studio

thisistinge.com

TINGE Studio is a Warsaw-based brand design studio run by Izabela Piotrowiak. TINGE creates branding, websites and packaging solutions for a diverse range of companies, and helps to transform organisations and businesses through profound strategic thinking and purposefully crafted design.

PP. 040–043, 130–131

TINT DESIGN
bytintlab.com

Tint Design is a multidisciplinary design studio based in Dubai, offering a variety of design services to clients all over the world. Their aim is to close the gap between functionality and aesthetic value through what they call Functional Beauty.

PP. 364–367

Todojunto & Ara Estudio
todojunto.net / araestudio.es

Todojunto is a design and communication studio based in Barcelona. Todojunto works with local and international educational and cultural institutions, and also frequently collaborates with Barcelona-based Ara Estudio, a graphic design and visual communication studio focused on branding, exhibition design, editorial and social media graphics.

PP. 064–069, 620–625

Tomi Leppänen Studio
tomileppanen.com

Tomi Leppänen is a Helsinki-based designer specialising in visual identities, art direction, objects, products, sounds, things, ideas and play.

PP. 100–103

Triangler Co., Ltd.
triangler.com.tw

Triangler is a young design company composed of design lovers, delivering the most suitable design service for brands. They believe that good design is collaboration based on mutual trust and positive knowledge sharing. Their services include brand and visual identity, graphic design, packaging design, web design, and event hosting.

PP. 060–063

Unifikat Design Studio
unifikat.com

Unifikat Design Studio is an experienced branding and art direction studio from Warsaw with the goal to help their clients to express themselves and their products. Their scope of work include visual identities and editorial design, packaging and photography for investments, companies, events or individual clients.

PP. 266–267

Violaine & Jérémy
violaineetjeremy.fr

Founded by Jérémy Schneider and Violaine Orsoni, Violaine & Jérémy is a multi-disciplinary creative studio in Paris focusing on graphic design, typography, and illustration. Dedicated to delivering beautiful messages, it believes in beauty, refinement, delicacy, and timelessness.

PP. 092–095

Vlad Boyko

behance.net/vladboyko2a302

Vlad Boyko is a graphic designer and media artist from Chernihiv. In his visual work, he focuses on typography and explores its entity and perception in different spaces and mediums, static and motion, digital and print. Vlad is inspired by his cultural background of constructionist, brutalist architecture and monumental art.

PP. 146–149

Vrints-Kolsteren

vrints-kolsteren.com

Vrints-Kolsteren is an Antwerp-based design studio founded by Vincent Vrints and Naomi Kolsteren. Working locally and internationally, it offers creative direction, photography, and graphic design services by engaging in ongoing partnerships and creating a network of creative collaborators.

PP. 024–029

WANGZHIHONG CO.

wangzhihong.com

Wang Zhi-Hong is a leading graphic designer from Taiwan and an AGI member. He has received numerous international accolades, including Kasai Kaoru's Choice Award at the HKDA Asia Design Awards, Best Book Design at the Paju Book Award, and Prize Nominee Works from the Tokyo Type Directors Club Annual Awards.

PP. 112–117, 244–245, 400–401

Acknowledgements

We would like to specially thank all the designers
and studios who are featured in this book for their
significant contribution towards its compilation.
We would also like to express our deepest gratitude
to our producers for their invaluable advice and
assistance throughout this project, as well as the
many professionals in the creative industry who were
generous with their insights, feedback, and time.
To those whose input was not specifically credited or
mentioned here, we truly appreciate your support.

Future Editions

If you wish to participate in viction:ary's future projects
and publications, please send your portfolio to:
we@victionary.com

Years Months Days

y-m-d.com

Intuitive and perceptive by nature, the work of Years Months Days Studio captures simplicity with beauty from offices in Melbourne, Munich and Berlin. The studio's team of designers, strategists, and art directors share a breadth of experience to create works that endure through collaboration with like-minded clients and creatives worldwide.

PP. 246–249

YumTang

behance.net/yumyang

YumTang currently lives in Beijing and is an independent food photographer. "Outside the appetite, inside the food" is how she defines her work, as she hopes to explore more possibilities of food by paying more attention to food itself and more possibilities after removing the edible attribute.

PP. 332-337

LA LLUNA DE LOTUS

LA LLUNA DE LOTUS
Art i poesia de la monja budista
Ōtagaki Rengetsu (1791–1875)

LA LUNA DE LOTO
Arte y poesía de la monja budista
Ōtagaki Rengetsu (1791–1875)

THE LOTUS MOON
Art and poetry of the Buddhist nun
Ōtagaki Rengetsu (1791–1875)